D0996040

The
Aspiring
Artist's
Journal

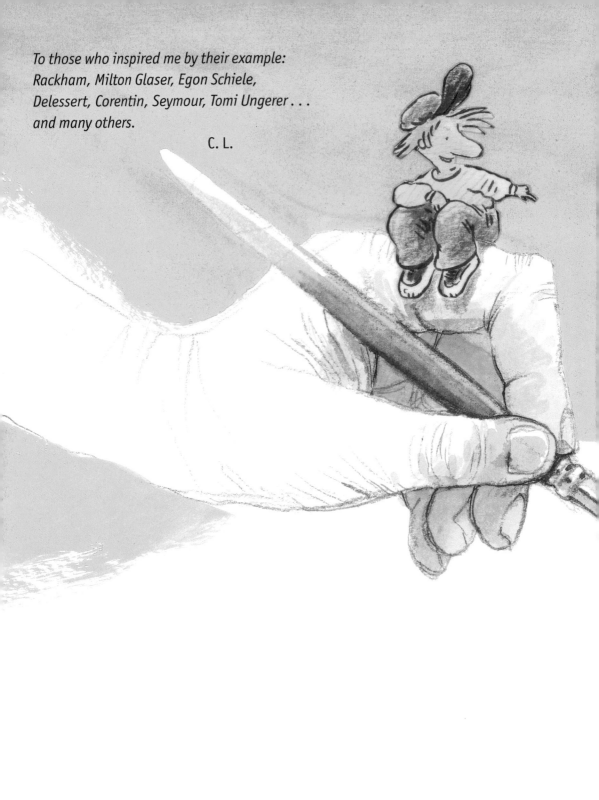

To those who inspired me by their example:
Rackham, Milton Glaser, Egon Schiele,
Delessert, Corentin, Seymour, Tomi Ungerer . . .
and many others.

C. L.

Claude Lapointe

Illustrated by Sylvette Guindolet

Aspiring
Artist's
Journal

Abrams Books for Young Readers
New York

My first drawing was of a train. Makes sense—I was born in a train station.

Later, I drew a lot in cafés. My grandmother ran a café in the train station where I was born.

In these places, I discovered "contact drawing," images that speak to people in such a way that two complete strangers looking at a drawing will start talking to each other.

"Who is that? Oh, I recognize him! Oh yeah, I definitely agree! Oh, that's interesting! I would love to see the rest . . ."

Viewers bring this kind of drawing to life.

In the 1970s, at a time when "anything goes," I founded the illustration studio in the School of Decorative Arts in Strasbourg. It was around this time that I started teaching "contact drawing."

I learned from, mentored, and watched some very talented young illustrators grow in their field.

The very first graduates are now older—they're fathers and mothers themselves. A lot of them are well-known illustrators or cartoonists. Others, newly graduated, often ask my advice on their projects.

Their diversity lets me explore the development of a narrative image, to examine its many aspects, and to study the relationship between words and images from a wonderfully rich and wide-reaching field of observation.

My partner and I thoroughly enjoyed creating a wide variety of exercises for this book: serious ones, funny ones, easy ones, difficult ones, some that we already know how to do, some that we might have done before, and some that we won't wait another second to start . . .

So pick up your pencils and join in!
Claude Lapointe

*"All the interest of art is in the beginning.
After the beginning, it is already the end."*

Pablo Picasso

*Trace the
hand you
sketch with.*

This is the hand
that will sketch
all the drawings
in this book.
Treat it with the
respect it
deserves.

A whole
year of
drawing
awaits!

Sketch a cat using a well-sharpened pencil, a moderately sharpened pencil, and a dull pencil. Which do you prefer?

Draw an inventive hairstyle for each face below.

A sharpened pencil lets you draw hair strand by strand, whereas a dull pencil is better for drawing lots of hair.

"Oh! Never to be freed from Numbers and Beings."
Charles Baudelaire

Sketch the number corresponding to whatever day of the month it is.

"Here was yellow, yellow and red, or azure when the rose flaps its wings; lights and colors filled the world, swelling and howling tenderly."

Hermann Hesse

Choose three different colored pencils. Fill in each square with one, two, or three colors. Feel free to superimpose them!

You will notice that some shades are warmer or colder, harsher or softer . . .

*"Every artist dips his brush in his own soul,
and paints his own nature into his pictures."*
Henry Ward Beecher

Which of the following three drawings do you like best? Is it the prettiest one? Or is it the one that's drawn the best?

"There is neither beautiful style, nor beautiful drawing, nor beautiful color; there is but one true beauty, the life that is revealed."

Auguste Rodin

I had no idea I had so many beautiful drawings!

Find an old drawing of yours that you're particularly proud of. Paste it, or a photocopy of it, here . . . or try to duplicate it.

"They call me a jolly man; my cheerfulness is my gift."
Gustave Nadaud

Draw some objects normally found around the house that can be used for the snowman's head.

You'll need something for its eyes, nose, mouth, hair, ears, neck . . . How about a carrot, a straw, some stones, a hat, some bits of wool, or other trinkets.

*"Winter kept us warm, covering
Earth in a forgetful snow . . ."*
T. S. (Thomas Stearns) Eliot

Don't wait for it to melt!
Using the objects you sketched, draw the kindest, the funniest,
or the scariest snowman you can. The choice is yours!

"A crooked log makes a straight fire."
Indian proverb

Draw a flame at the end of the match, the wick, the branch, and the bail of hay.

The fire in a drawing can't burn you,
the water in a drawing can't get you wet,
the whip in a drawing can't hurt you.
But are you sure that a drawing is harmless?

"The mind is not a vessel to be filled but a fire to be kindled."
Plutarch

Light a big fire in the hearth.

Measure the exact length of this line.

Is it difficult?
Now take some thread and
position it directly over the
line; once you get to the end,
cut it and measure it.

GRRR

Using the thread from Day 12, trace the silhouette of an animal of your choice. Then glue the thread onto the paper and complete the drawing.

Sketch a person opening a door (and not closing it).

I turn my head to one side when I enter my home. Once I'm inside, I turn my head to the other side. Who am I? *Find the answer on Day 20.*

"Laughter is peculiar to humans."
Henri Bergson

Draw one mouth laughing, one shouting,
and one "sewn shut."

"Without poets, without artists, men would soon weary of nature's monotony."

Guillaume Apollinaire

Place a still life (one or more objects: a vase, a stuffed animal . . .) in the room farthest away from the one in which you're drawing. Take the time to really look at the still life, then return to the other room and draw it.

Come back from time to time, when your memory fails. Compare the still life to your finished drawing.

I don't know if my drawing will improve, but my health certainly will!

"Some memories are realities, and are better than anything that can ever happen to one again."
Willa Cather

Two people meet.
One has a vast memory,
the other a wild imagination.

Draw what's happening inside their heads. Do you think they would get along, or at least understand each other?

A a

This font comes from the Elzevir family. Its name is Times.

I'm following your advice to the letter!

A bit of typography.

Write the letters "B" and "b" using the same font as the "A" and "a" on this page.

It will be easier to draw it in large format.

"And after all, what is a lie?
'Tis but the truth in masquerade."
Lord Byron

Words can lie,
but images can deceive just as well!

blue
yellow

I'm a giant!

Think of ways you can
illustrate opposites.
Drawings aren't always
what they say they are!

Day 20

*"The cat ran in the snow; when it came back,
it was wearing white boots."*
Traditional French children's song

*Draw a black cat
in the snow.*

Answer to the riddle from Day 14: a key.

"Art evokes the mystery without which the world would not exist."

René Magritte

Hmm . . .
an odd
corner!

Draw a white cat in the snow using correction fluid.

The good king Henri IV and his beautiful queen from the
15th century can't keep their heads uncovered any longer.

*Cover their heads with a hat from the
time period, or invent one of your own.*

Influenced by a painting by
Pisanello (1410–1420).

"A face: If it isn't a secret door, it's at least a point of entry. We decorate and shape it for visitors' eyes."
Kobo Abe

Draw a face that corresponds best to the following two hats.

I am white as well as green, red, or black. One has to climb me in order to come down. Who am I?
Find out on Day 31.

*"I may not have gone where I intended to go,
but I think I have ended up where I intended to be."*
Douglas Adams

*Can you draw the imprint of
this sole on the muddy path?*

*"The uncomfortable Roman shoe paved
the way for great stone-laden paths."*
Montesquieu

These two won't get very far barefoot.
Hurry up and put shoes on them!

*"The first step, my son, that one takes in this world
is the one on which the rest of our days depend."*

Voltaire

Finish drawing the bodies of these two
couples so that they can finish their dance.

*This musician will only play
if there are dancers . . .*

"A donkey cannot differentiate between sound and music."
French proverb

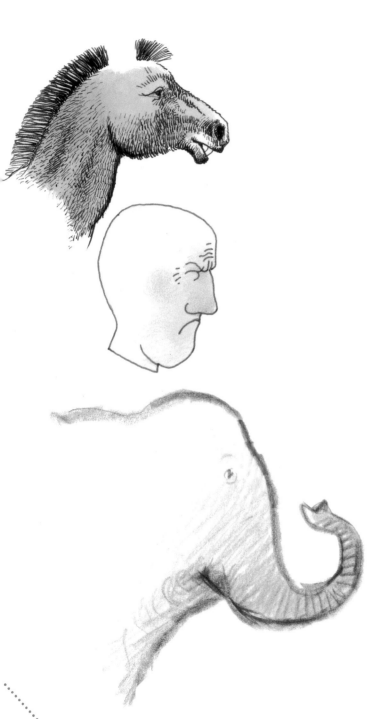

Draw a pair of ears on these three avid listeners.

"Music that does not depict is just noise."
D'Alembert

dance

rock

death metal

deep house

funk

house

punk

rap

classical

Match these musical styles with a color
or object that best corresponds to each.

"I once said that it wasn't sufficient to hear music; one had to see it as well."

Igor Stravinsky

Draw a musical instrument that can be played while walking.

"The true work of art is but a shadow of the divine perfection."

Michelangelo

If at this point you wish to abandon drawing for music . . . let's start learning some notes.

Draw an F key, a C key, a whole note in C, a half note in E, a sixteenth note in G, and a sixty-fourth note in B.

Answer to the riddle on Day 23: a ski slope.

"Fools make feasts, and wise men eat them."
Benjamin Franklin

Draw your favorite food on the plate below.

"Two gluttons never dine from the same plate."
French proverb

Recipes are useful, but when they're accompanied by illustrations, they're practically foolproof!

Illustrate the recipe below using clear and simple sketches.

1

2

3

4

5

6

15 minutes of prep time; each crepe takes 4 minutes to cook . . .

For 6 people, 3 cups of flour, 3 eggs, 3 cups of milk, salt . . .

CREPE INSTRUCTIONS
1. Pour the flour into a mixing bowl.
2. Break the eggs in the middle of the bowl.
3. Add 3 pinches of salt.
4. Mix everything together while adding the milk, little by little.
5. When the batter reaches a thin and smooth consistency, cover it.

*"Take a shortcut to the table
and the long way to work."*
Gaelic proverb

7

9

8

10

6. Set it aside for 2 hours.
7. Make the crepes in a greased skillet.
8. Flip them over.
9. Keep them warm between 2 plates in the oven.
10. Serve them rolled up and dusted with sugar.

Double, double, toil and trouble;
Fire, burn; and caldron, bubble.
Fillet of a fenny snake,
In the caldron boil and bake;
Eye of newt, and toe of frog,
Wool of bat, and tongue of dog,
Adder's fork, and blind-worm's sting,
Lizard's leg, and howlet's wing—
For a charm of powerful trouble,
Like a hell-broth boil and bubble.

William Shakespeare, from *Macbeth*

Draw a wicked witch
preparing a cauldron of the
nastiest brew imaginable.

"To Shakespeare, all the world's a stage; to me, it's a kitchen where people come and go."
Arnold Wesker

*Two diners sit side by side
at a restaurant.*

The first diner is polite, at ease,
smiling, a bit of a snob.
The other one is uncouth, a real lout.
Try to imagine them in action.

"The best gestures are the natural ones.
The ones we learn always look fake."
Sacha Guitry

This poor waiter must cross the restaurant balancing a tray crammed with plates, glasses, and bottles.

"A simple window can also be seen as a frame to the most beautiful painting."
Jacques Charpentreau

Draw the stores on a lively street, where a restaurant sits among some stores you might like to visit.

Framing brings out the best of a landscape.

"A tailor's art does not depend solely on scissors and measuring tape."

Lu Yu

You, the illustrator, have just moved into your new workshop.

Draw your shop sign, as well as that of your neighbor, the writer.

"With practice, a craft develops almost on its own, and all the more easily when one focuses on something other than technique."

Paul Gauguin

Draw a suspended shop sign, the kind that can be spotted from far away.

The Illustrator

The Writer

A cheese store's shop sign

"Experience is the name we give to our mistakes."
Oscar Wilde

Do you recall the
last stupid thing
you, your friend,
or your sibling did?

*Have fun
depicting it below.*

This jam lover needs your help.
How can he reach the jar of jam? Draw your proposed solution.

One solution appears on Day 60.

"He who sees nothing has nothing to say."
Jean de La Fontaine

Take a dozen nuts and spread them out on the floor in front of you. Choose one with your eyes and look at it closely. Without touching it, try to draw it as accurately as possible.

You must focus on it for a long time in order to notice its peculiarities.

"The eye of a human being is a microscope, which makes the world seem bigger than it really is."

Kahlil Gibran, from "A Handful of Sand on the Shore"

Peer through a cardboard cylinder and look around the room.

Choose three different views and draw them in the holes below.

"Love looks not with the eyes, but with the mind;
And therefore is winged Cupid painted blind."
William Shakespeare

Draw the eyes of your girlfriend or boyfriend, or the person you dream of. Put your heart into the task!

"Life is full of absurdities that do not need to appear plausible. And do you know why? Because they're true."
Luigi Pirandello

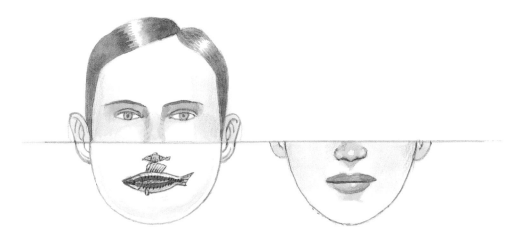

Finish the drawing on the right in the same style as the one on the left.

"We will be known forever by the tracks we leave."
Native American proverb

*This skier won't get very far
if you don't complete the drawing!
Don't forget the tracks she
leaves behind her.*

Guess whose footprints these are. When you've figured out which animal left them, draw it!

"The last step depends on the first; the first step depends on the last."

René Daumal

Track A

Track B

Track C

"Be like a duck. Calm on the surface, but always paddling like the dickens underneath."

Michael Caine

Enliven this mallard with a bit of color and fill in the missing letters of its loud quacks.

"I bend but do not break."
Jean de La Fontaine,
from "The Oak and the Reed"

Day 50

Two frightened frogs
dive into the water.
Now draw the pond
and its surroundings,
and make the frogs croak.

"When they dream, they take on noble attitudes of the great sphinxes stretched out in the depths of solitude, who seem to fall into a sleep of endless dreams."

Charles Baudelaire

This tiger forgot to get dressed!
Give him his stripes, or invent
new ones...

"To a mouse, a cat is a tiger. But to a tiger, a cat is a mouse."
Persian proverb

Draw a cat
a quarter of the size
of the tiger, a mouse
a quarter of the size
of the cat, and a flea
a sixteenth of the
size of the mouse.

"What right does one have to put birds in cages?"
Victor Hugo

Put a wild tiger in this cage.

It if saddens you to see it locked up,
try to sketch the key and free it!

"Man needs his freedom like a body needs a soul."
Charles Baudelaire

A bird takes flight.
Try to capture this
magical moment.

"Principles for the Development of a Complete Mind: Study the science of art. Study the art of science. Develop your senses—especially learn how to see. Realize that everything connects to everything else."

Leonardo da Vinci

Choose a color for lightning, the sound of a violin, footsteps crunching in the snow, and a dog barking.

Then ask other people which color they associate with each.

"A fly cannot enter a closed mouth."
Prosper Mérimée

The door to this house is very small.
Which animals can pass through it?

*Draw an animal that can
easily fit through the door
and one that's just a bit too big . . .*

"When the cat is away, the mice will play."
Creole proverb

Draw a family of mice dancing.

"A book that doesn't address itself to the majority, in quantity and intelligence, is a stupid book."
Charles Baudelaire

You may have come across a drawing that you didn't quite understand. Try to find it again, or find another one (in an art book or a schoolbook).

Glue it or copy it here. Are other readers as perplexed as you?

These two must have a good reason for fighting.

Imagine what words they might be exchanging, and write them in the bubbles using two different sets of handwriting.

"Read, every day, something no one else is reading. Think, every day, something no one else is thinking. Do, every day, something no one else would be silly enough to do. It is bad for the mind to continually be part of unanimity."

Christopher Morley

Twenty-nine people are sledding down a hill. Try to sketch them all.

One possible solution for the little glutton on Day 42.

"Hope is a loan from happiness."
Joseph Joubert

Hope cannot be illustrated,
but it can be evoked.

*Try to draw a color,
animal, or person
that says hope to you.*

"Scaffolding does not a building make."
Napoleon III

With eyes half closed, she
builds her castle . . .

*Draw her dream
house in the
bubble.*

STOCK
◿ : 14
□ : 80

With this supply of stones and
half stones, construct the castle
exactly as it appears in the model.

Our little friend has already laid the first stone for you . . .

"The moon was calm and flecked the ocean waves."
Victor Hugo

On a beautiful evening, the moon, hang glider, and pteranodon fill the sky.

But they're not really there unless their shadows appear . . .

"The man who has no imagination has no wings."
Muhammad Ali

Except for
birds, draw
some objects
that have wings.

*"An idea, like a ghost, must be spoken to
a little before it will explain itself."*
Charles Dickens

*Draw the ghost rider of your dreams,
or your nightmares . . .*

Take your sketchbook, along with a pencil or
felt-tip pen, to your room and lie down on your bed.

*Draw the first thing you see
when you get up.*

*I'm sorry,
can you
repeat that?*

*"There is nothing in the world as soft and yielding as water,
and yet nothing can better overcome the hard and strong."*

Lao Tzu

Brainstorm
eight types
of weather,
and sketch
each.

*This gardener seems to be somewhat clueless.
Try to guess what's going to happen to him.*

"The waterfalls cascade downward like spirited horses, their manes full of foam and the hues of the rainbow."
Ismaïl Kadare

The ways in which water moves aren't easy to illustrate.

Try to draw boiling water, a waterfall, or water splashing!

"A poet is a world enclosed in a man."
Victor Hugo

Choose a poem.
Now illustrate what it means to you.

"A map of the world that does not include Utopia is not worth glancing at."
Oscar Wilde

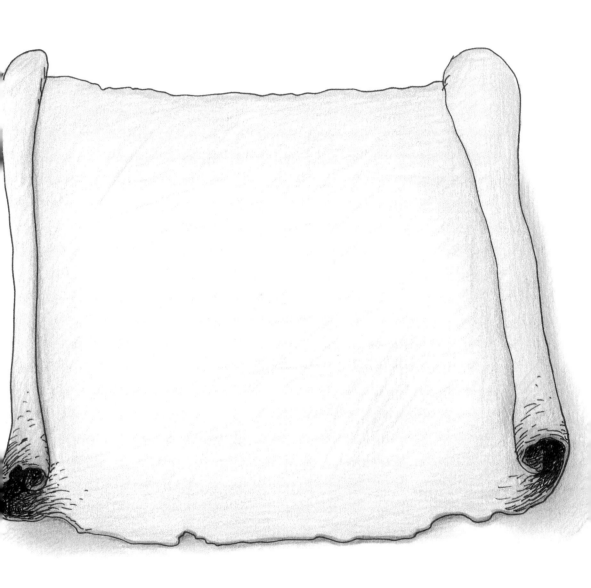

The country of Utopia exists, and the proof is that you're going to make a map of it, with its cities, capital, forests, rivers, and mountains . . .

"Geniuses are like thunderstorms. They go against the wind, terrify people, cleanse the air."

Søren Kierkegaard

Without leaving
a single corner
of the page blank,

*draw a thick,
heavy rainstorm.*

"An open umbrella is a beautiful, enclosed sky."
Xavier Forneret

Fill the underside
of this umbrella
with everything your
vivid imagination
can dream up.

"Keep an eye fixed on the summit, but don't forget to look in front of you."
René Daumal

This mountaineer is far from the summit.

Draw him at five different points along the mountain, finishing, of course, at the top!

"Love can make you dizzy, but as intolerable as it may feel, it's still an infinite delight."

Hubert Aquin

Do you suffer from vertigo?

Draw yourself in a situation in which you're most vulnerable to height.

. . . and my hat is beyond ruined!

"When I am finishing a picture, I hold some God-made object up to it—a rock, a flower, the branch of a tree, or my hand—as a final test. If the painting stands up beside a thing man cannot make, the painting is authentic. If there's a clash between the two, it's bad art."

Marc Chagall

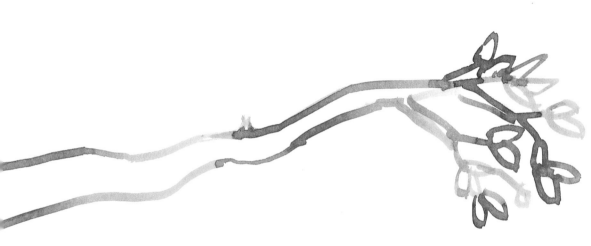

At a distance

The leaves

The berries

Using these detailed drawings as a guide, sketch some mistletoe on the tree branch.

"A tree knocked over by the wind has more branches than roots."
Chinese proverb

*Try to sketch
the visible parts
of these plants.*

"The human face has always been the greatest landscape."
Colette

The profile of a person lying down can become a kind of landscape.

Imagine how the nose, chin, and lips can be transformed into mountains, rivers, trees, and prairies . . .

"No occupation is so delightful to me as the culture of the earth, and no culture comparable to that of the garden."

Thomas Jefferson

Continue the landscape from the previous page and draw in a gardener who plants and waters the land . . .

Add buds to the following branches,

either by looking them up or reproducing them from memory.

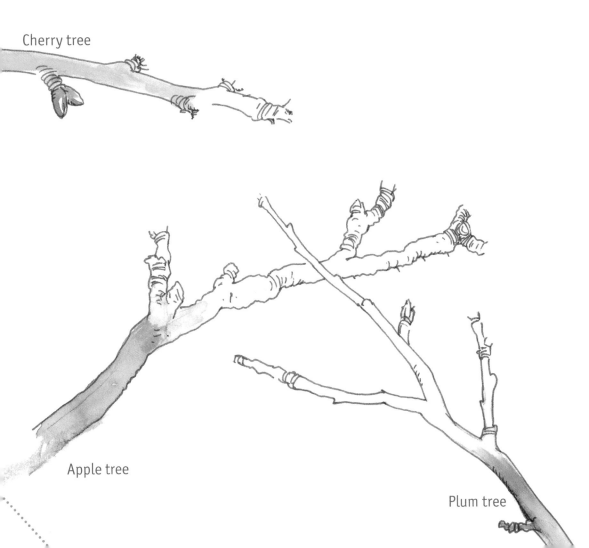

Cherry tree

Apple tree

Plum tree

"In spite of all the refinements of civilization that conspired to make art—the dizzying perfection of the string quartet or the sprawling grandeur of Fragonard's canvases—beauty was savage . . . Beauty was a Savage Garden."

Anne Rice

Imagine this abandoned garden overgrown with herbs, flowers, vegetables, ivy, and shrubs.

"Let us admire the great masters, not imitate them."
Victor Hugo

Have you ever copied a drawing before? Do you think it helps you to draw better?

If yes, reserve this blank space for the next time
you visit a museum or art gallery and are inspired
by a painting, even if it's completely unknown.

It's you
and me
once more!

**Self-Portrait with a Pipe,
by Vincent van Gogh**

"Art which has life doesn't reproduce the past; it continues it."
Auguste Rodin

 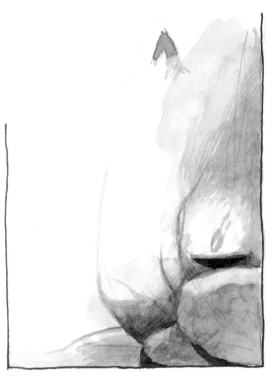

This man is painting.
Prehistoric people also painted.

*Draw him standing upright in his cave,
painting on the wall . . .*

Do people draw better nowadays?

"Those who cannot remember the past are destined to repeat it."
George Santayana

Draw the letter *C*
like the letter *D*
on the next page,
or however else
you imagine it.

Do you
know how
this crazy
story ends?

Uh, yeah . . .
unless you've
changed the
ending.

Do you recall having done the same
stupid thing or made the same error
more than once?

Try to illustrate it.

"If you were born lucky, even your rooster will lay eggs."
Russian proverb

Construct a sentence using the above proverb as a model, changing the animal and the action. Illustrate it below in a humorous style.

"The spectator is a prince who rejoices in his incognito status everywhere he goes."
Charles Baudelaire

Draw a person without letting yourself be seen.

Hide behind a peephole, a fence, blinds, or even harder, peer through a keyhole. It's a bad thing to do, of course, but for this one time, the author of this book, who assumes responsibility for the consequences of your actions, authorizes it.

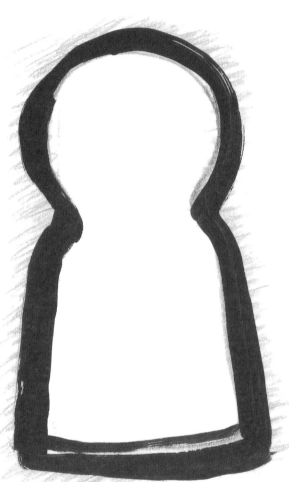

 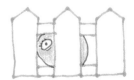 

"No matter how sharp your eyesight may be, you still can't see yourself from behind."

Chinese proverb

Try your best to draw yourself as you appear from behind.

Place a photograph or drawing of an animal or person in front of you, using it as a model.

Draw the picture in reverse, so that the right side becomes the left side.

Once you've done that, check the accuracy of your drawing by holding it up to a mirror.

Dagobert I
c. 600–638 CE

"The good king Dagobert put his underwear on backward."
Traditional French song

"Habits are safer than rules; you don't have to watch them. And you don't have to keep them either. They keep you."

Frank Crane

You have a
bad habit,
don't you?

*Poke fun at it
by way of a
satirical drawing.*

You might just get
rid of it, or, if the
drawing is good
enough, you might
take pride in it!

Anyone
who draws a
caricature of
me will have
to deal with
me face to
face!

"Hasten slowly, and without losing heart, put your work twenty times upon the anvil. Polish it and repolish it continuously; add to it occasionally and erase often."
Nicolas Boileau

Redraw sketch number 4 of the mountaineer from Day 74 by enlarging it and improving it.

Place some tracing paper over the sketch and correct any detectable flaws. Then paste a second piece of tracing paper over the first and improve your drawing even more. By the time you place a third sheet of tracing paper over it, you will have attained perfection! (Unless you think you never needed any corrections in the first place!)

When you're a perfectionist like me, you never count your rough drafts!

"It is always a silly thing to give advice, but to give good advice is fatal."

Oscar Wilde

Draw two people listening to the professor: One of them seems to accept his advice, the other seems doubtful.

"A man who thinks highly of himself and his appearance forgets that he is also seen from behind."

Saying

Finish the sketch.
Feel free to add words, if necessary.

"To catch a salmon one must lose a minnow."
Chinese proverb

Draw a big fish swallowing a small fish,

preceded by a bigger fish swallowing
the second fish, preceded by an even
bigger fish swallowing the third fish . . .
keep going until you run out of room.

"When the fish is caught, its net is forgotten. When an idea takes form, the words used to convey it are of little use."

Zhuang Zi

What do you make of the following drawings?

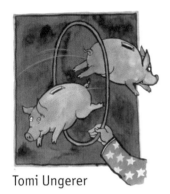

Tomi Ungerer

Laville

"A face: If it isn't a secret door, it's at least a point of entry. We decorate and shape it for visitors' eyes."

Kobo Abe

Apply makeup to the following faces for a party, carnival, Halloween, going incognito, or any other occasion of your choice . . .

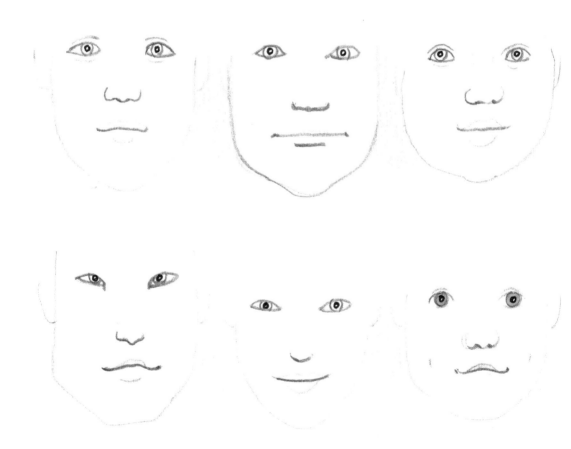

"Black children and white children both have red blood."

Pierre Osenat

Draw the sketch of a poster against racism.

*"It's not enough to take steps that culminate in a goal.
Each step must itself be a goal and a step likewise."*
Goethe, from *Conversations*

To become an illustrator or cartoonist,
you must overcome many obstacles.
Below are some goals that you can check off
and adapt, according to your personal ideas.

Remember certain scenes to make sketches of them.
Make a sketch before a final drawing.
Learn to draw a hand drawing.
Master the art of drawing letters and numbers.
Have the patience to start the same drawing three or more times.
Be sure of your progress.
Choose a beautiful drawing over one that makes you think.
Learn how to draw a caricature.
Choose a drawing that makes you think over a beautiful one.
Draw an exact portrait.

Avoid
over-
working!

"When you're led by the blind, you end up in a ditch."

Malagasy proverb

Look closely at the expressions of the people in this painting.

What feelings can you make out?
What is the underlying idea of it?

The Parable of the Blind, *by Pieter Brueghel*

"If wishes came true, poor men would be princes."
Jean de La Véprie

You shook the bottle of juice so forcefully that a genie popped out.

How does she or he look?

The genie will grant you
three wishes, but only if you
know how to draw them . . .

(1)

(2)

These images are extracts from Heinrich Hoffmann's *Slovenly Peter*.

Draw the missing scene.

You will encounter it later in this book.

(3)

"A crow trying to imitate a duck drowns upon entering the water."
Mongolian proverb

Illustrate this quote

or invent a scene in which one animal is in trouble because it's imitating another animal.

"A tree in one day cannot grow, nor does it fall from a single blow."
Jacob Cat

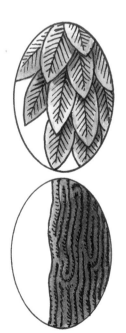

Draw a tree with all its leaves and the rough surface of its trunk.

You will be tired once you're done, and perhaps surprised and happy with your results.

"A tree passes by; a man looks at it and notices that its hair is green."

Robert Sabatier

In fairy tales, trees are often characters with magical powers. Draw your own tree character.

"Trees are the earth's endless effort to speak to the listening heaven."
Rabindranath Tagore

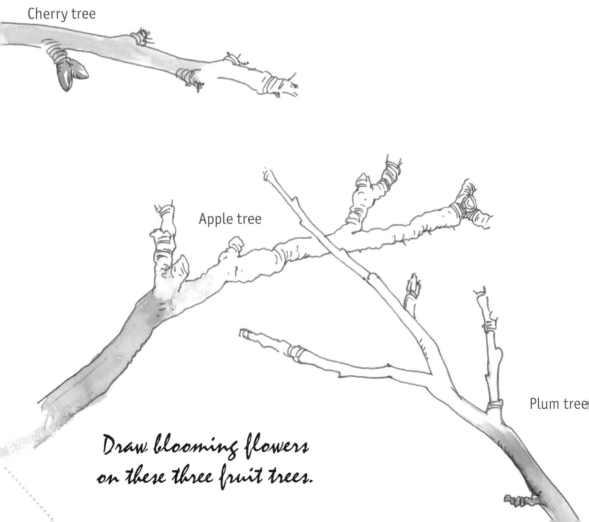

Cherry tree

Apple tree

Plum tree

*Draw blooming flowers
on these three fruit trees.*

"Do you have a message for me?
You can tell me, I'm discreet.
Is your greenery a secret?
Is your perfume a language?"
Alfred de Musset

Cut out photos of flowers from a catalogue and assemble them here to make a big bouquet.

"The horizon is in the eyes, and not in reality."
Angel Ganivet

Draw three trees, three road signs, and three cars along this road.

This man is returning home to his blue house.

Draw him at various other places in this drawing. You can add several passersby.

"Shadows of palaces, of domes and of spires,
Of towers and of castle-keeps, of steeples, of bastilles,
Of battlements, of kiosks and of sharp minarets,
Of outlines of ramparts, of gardens, of forests,
Of spirals, of arches, of parks, of colonnades,
Of obelisks, of bridges, of doorways and of arcades,
It bustles and grows, grips as it rises,
Curves, recoils or deepens or expands."

Alfred de Vigny

I live
here

Draw a map of your neighborhood.
Add monuments or curiosities if there are any.

"Conception, my boy, fundamental brain work, is what makes all the difference in art."
Dante Gabriel Rossetti

Draw the passenger in the taxi after decoding the message and figuring out his or her identity.

"One of the greatest discoveries a man makes, one of his greatest surprises, is to find he can do what he was afraid he couldn't."

Henry Ford

Wow! There were already cars way back then!

Draw the car you always dreamed of driving.

"There is no horse that can't be fitted with a saddle."
Proverb

When this man wants to get around, he gets on his bike. What would he have done in the Middle Ages, and what will he do in the year 3333?

Here is the missing scene from Day 101.

"Cities have always been the fireplaces of civilization, whence light and heat radiated out into the dark."

Theodore Parker

Create a city using houses
cut from the pages of magazines.
Don't forget skyscrapers!

"The most beautiful thing we can experience is the mysterious."
Albert Einstein

Try to guess what is on the other side of the wall. The answer will come tomorrow.

"Art is not a mirror held up to reality, but a hammer with which to shape it."
Bertolt Brecht

Draw what you imagined was behind the wall yesterday.

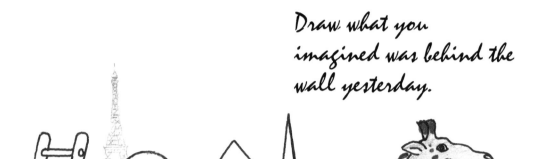

"A pessimist only sees the dark side of the clouds, and mopes; a philosopher sees both sides and shrugs; an optimist doesn't see the clouds at all—he's walking on them."

Leonard L. Levinson

A perfect white cloud and a dark, menacing cloud pass high above the city. Bring them to life.

"Inside my empty bottle I was constructing a lighthouse while all the others were making ships."

Charles Simic

Place the Statue of Liberty in one of these bottles and a monument of your choice in the other.

Create a statue or
monument for your
village or neighborhood.

Draw a person next to it,
in order to show the scale.

I'm the right scale.

"The finest works of art are precious, among other reasons, because they make it possible for us to know, if only imperfectly and for a while, what it actually feels like to think subtly and feel nobly."

Aldous Huxley

Draw the letter *F* in bricks, like the *E* on the facing page.

Paste a pretty flower to this page. Next to it, draw a magnified detail of it that interests you the most.

"At every step the child should be allowed to meet the real experience of life; the thorns should never be plucked from his roses."

Ellen Key

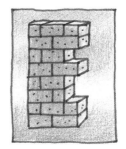

An aggressive, prickly, suffocating carnivorous plant attacks a hiker.

You witness the scene.
Draw what happened.

"Work leads to wealth.
Work hard, poor poets!
With perseverance, the caterpillar
Becomes a rich butterfly."
Guillaume Apollinaire

The caterpillar (a) undergoes metamorphosis to become a pupa (b), which transforms into a butterfly (c). Complete the drawing by adding details.

The butterfly shown here is called a tortoiseshell butterfly.

"Have you seen but a bright lily grow,
Before rude hands have touched it?
Have you marked but the fall o' the snow
Before the soil hath smutched it? . . .
O so white! O so soft! O so sweet is she!"

Ben Jonson

Look closely at a sprig of lily of the valley.
Now draw it in a stylish but simplified way.

This is called a pictogram.
Glue some other pictograms to this page,
next to your drawing.

"We do not imitate, but are a model to others."
Pericles

Using your drawing from yesterday, make a stencil and then create a sheet of fabric by copying it over and over again.

To make your stencil:

Trace your drawing
on a box or a piece
of plastic. Now cut the
drawing out, so that
paint can fill in the shape.
Using a small paintbrush
or piece of cloth dipped in
paint, do several tests.

To make the fabric:

Repeat your drawing over and
over on a piece of white fabric.
Glue a swatch of your
creation to this page!

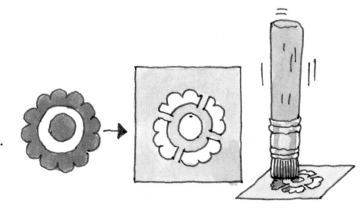

"Clothes make the man."
Saying

Fashion design: Design a casual outfit you can wear out with your friends.

You can paste some swatches of fabric for your outfit next to your drawing.

"Fashion is not something that exists in dresses only. Fashion is in the sky, in the street, fashion has to do with ideas, the way we live, what is happening."

Coco Chanel

Fashion design:
Design an outfit for a
special occasion or for a
famous fashion designer.

*"The artist should never try to be popular.
Rather the public should be more artistic."*
Oscar Wilde

*Draw some accessories
to go with the casual
outfit you designed
on Day 124.*

Take your pick:
gloves, purse, sneakers,
shoes, leggings, bandana,
baseball cap, belt,
suspenders, tie, etc.

"Knowledge is always accompanied with accessories of emotion and purpose."
Alfred North Whitehead

Draw the accessories that will accompany your fancy designer outfit.

(They can be the same as the ones on the preceding page: purse, gloves, etc.)

*"Everyone must yield to fashion
The crazy man introduces it
And the wise man follows suit."*
Legrand, song

Choose two periods
in history that you're
particularly fond of.
Draw yourself dressed
in outfits dating from
those times.

Hello, my compatriot!

"The past and the future are constantly joining together, leaving only the present."

Dom Deschamps

Anachronism.
Choose two far-apart periods of time.

Create an outfit that combines the styles of the different time periods.

Then ask someone what he or
she likes most about the outfit.

I've always
been ahead
of my time.

Day 130

A cat and a book.
Make one or two drawings
featuring them both.

"A good book must always create a bond between the person who wrote it and the one reading it."
Laure Conan

Every reader is the director of the book he or she is reading.
"Morgan looked sunny in her light-colored dress."

Draw your version of Morgan and ask a friend to draw his or her own version.

Morgan looked sunny in her light-colored dress.

Morgan looked sunny in her light-colored dress.

Day 132

It isn't easy to draw someone at the table.
Using today's quote as a guide,

*draw a diner or a reader
from four different approaches.*

"What good is a book without pictures or words,
Alice wondered."

Lewis Carroll, from *Alice's Adventures in Wonderland*

Create your own Alice.

You may want to read or re-read
Alice's Adventures in Wonderland
to help you.

r John Tenniel   **Lola Anglada**   **Barry Moser**   **Arthur Rackham**   **Charles Robinson**

"Inanimate objects, do you have a soul?"
Alphonse de Lamartine

When you get angry, do you ever take it out on an object? Create such a scene, drawing the object as though it was a person.

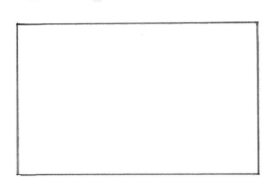

Draw the letter *G*
like the letter *H*
on Day 135.

"Bizarre, bizarre, you said bizarre . . ."
Jules Romains, from *Doctor Knock*

Place an object somewhere where it normally doesn't belong.

If it makes someone smile, you win. If you incite an intense philosophical or existential discussion, even better.

"A good man never goes far enough, a bad one always goes too far, such that both miss their goal."

Morris West

Here is a lawn bowling court.

Draw a player who's excited, furious, and gesticulating wildly, fearing that his ball might go too far.

Next to him, draw a shy player whose ball definitely won't reach its destination!

"A good archer nails the target before pulling the bow."

Zhao Buzhi

The lawn bowler's partners anxiously watch where their balls might land.

"A monkey never looked more like an animal than when dressed in man's clothing."

Indian proverb

Animals are often given human attributes in stories or fairy tales.

Draw some animals that you remember from your childhood.

Complete the double mask above,
showing two opposing faces.
One is smiling, calm, and kind;
the other is sad, angry, or aggressive.

Finish the drawing of this trapeze artist by pasting on a face from a catalog or a photograph of a friend.

"I don't want to be called 'the greatest' or 'one of the greatest'; let other guys claim to be the best. I just want to be known as a clown because to me that's the height of my profession. It means you can do everything—sing, dance, and above all, make people laugh."

Red Skelton

Three clowns—a sad clown, a bland clown, and a funny clown—are in love with the trapeze artist.

Try to imagine their attitudes and facial expressions.

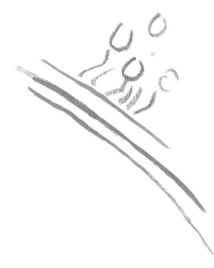

*"Time is a circus,
always packing up
and moving away."*
Ben Hecht

The New Circus
is waiting for you:
Draw a juggler in the
middle of his act and
spectators in the stands.

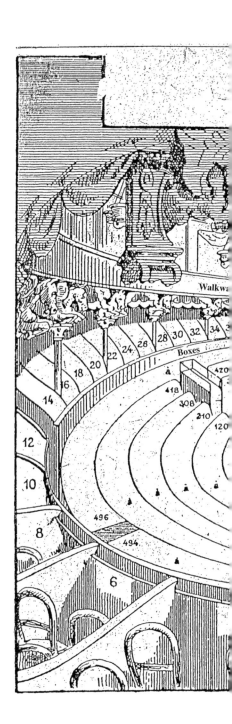

Thirteenth
lesson . . .
be humble.

NEW CIRCUS
3,500 seats

Orchestra

Walkway   Walkway

Boxes

Boxes

Front row   Front row

Front row

Entrance

Boxes

Each box
has five seats

Copy the mouth, nose, right eye, and left eye below on four separate pieces of tracing paper; now transfer them onto the face below.

Do the activity again to create some other different types of faces.

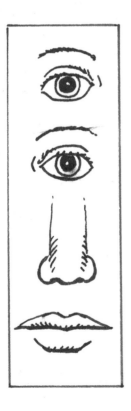

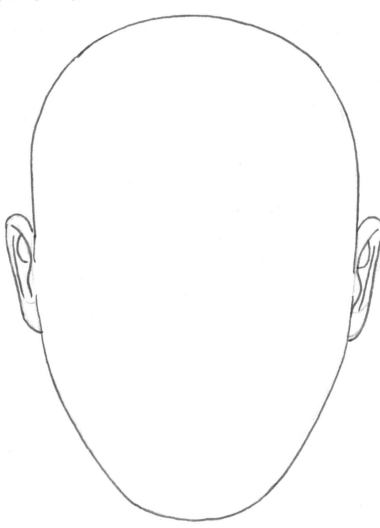

Here's a trick: Trace these facial features with a wax pencil; next, turn over the tracing paper, position it correctly, and rub (the pencil leaves a trace of the facial feature).

ME

Today's the day for your self-portrait. Apply yourself and try not to get too worked up!

How is it that I see myself so often and yet know myself so little?

At the outdoor café . . .

Three female (or male) patrons
wearing sunglasses watch a handsome young man
(or a beautiful young woman) walk past.

Give each patron a different facial expression.

The "medium close-up" is a composition
in which people are depicted in full and
in which the focus is on them, not on the
surroundings.

"Will you love me in December as you do in May?
Will you love me in the good old-fashioned way?"
James J. Walker

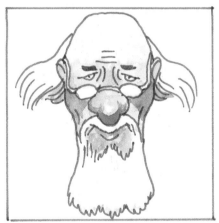

Play with the idea of time.
Draw the young boy as an old man and then draw
the old man as he might have looked as a young boy.

You can replace the faces already drawn with passport
photos of you or your family . . .

*"I fell asleep
While thinking of him
And saw him appear before me.
Oh, if I knew it was a dream
I'd never have awakened."*

Ono No Komachi, from *Poems*

The Mona Lisa fell asleep. She's dreaming.

In the style of Leonardo da Vinci, draw the Mona Lisa with her eyes closed.

"Ask yourself whether the dream of heaven and greatness should be waiting for us in our graves—or whether it should be ours here and now and on this earth."

Ayn Rand

How would you draw your idea of heaven on earth?

Dubout,
1905–1976
Caricaturist

"One derives greater pleasure from hoping for something than from obtaining it."
Jean-Jacques Rousseau

Paste one or two drawings here that you wish you could have painted yourself.

Don't forget the names of the painters.

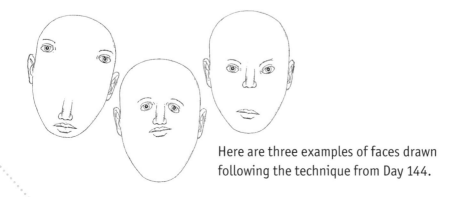

Here are three examples of faces drawn following the technique from Day 144.

"If someone understands what I'm saying, then I'm not expressing myself very well."
Jean-Luc Godard

Draw something that only you can understand.

It's not easy, is it?
An image is made up of a place, a person, and an action. Create an image in which the expressions, objects, and characters don't really go together and are only comprehensible to you.

Ah . . . yes . . . yes.
You have perfectly captured
the profound forces of human
nature plagued by a legitimate
need to let everything go . . .

"Life is a journey with coattails sweeping behind, erasing its tracks."
Louis Aragon

Draw an image using a pencil . . .
now gently erase it.
Enjoy the traces that it leaves behind.

Day 153

*"The cherries had enough of looking toward the ground
So they looked toward the sky
And became red balloons."*

André Clair

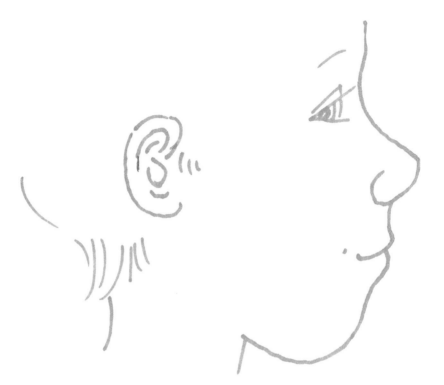

Dangle some cherries from the ears of this little girl, as though they were earrings.

But these are cherries!

Well, yes, but in a single movement, they become jewelry!

JEWELRY $20

Illustrate each of the following
expressions any way you like.

Happy as a clam

Under the weather

Splitting hairs

Day 155

Draw a newspaper or magazine headline denouncing inequality.

Draw an identical person to the one below, but smaller;

behind that one, draw an even smaller one, and so on,
until the edge of the page. In front of him, draw a larger
(but otherwise identical) person, followed by another larger one,
and an even larger one, and so on . . .

"A fool set off running for the whole of Russia, to see his countryman, and in turn, to be seen."
Leo Tolstoy, from *Ivan the Fool*

"He who crawls never falls."
Stoyan Mikhailovski

Draw two puppets,

one of which is bowing to the other with bitterness and scorn.
Exaggerate their attitudes and expressions.

A person is hidden behind each of the four columns, spying on the others.

Find the best position for each.
(Sketch them first on another sheet of paper.)

"On the stage, one must have reality and one must have joy."
John Millington Synge

Sketch:

Draw the encounter between the two dog walkers in the third box.
In the fourth box, draw their fall!

"Be attentive spectators when you may not be actors."
José Enrique Rodo

Imagine two people at a distance.

Draw their interaction based on gestures and facial expressions alone.

Day 161

Draw a poor little piece of lettuce standing his ground against the voracious snail.

"Botany is the art of drying up plants between sheets of paper and insulting them in Greek and in Latin."
Alphonse Karr

BOTANICAL PLATE

PLX

FLOWER DISCOVERED BY:

Invent a flower.

Draw it and give it a scholarly name.
Write the name in calligraphy, in your best handwriting.

"An attic should always be filled with sunshine."
Proverb

Fill this attic with boxes, trunks, and random objects.

Take a good look at an attic when it is dark and illuminated only by a skylight or small window. Note how the light hits the objects. One of the functions of color is for emphasis, to create an atmosphere, much like spotlights do.

"The man who has not anything to boast of but his illustrious ancestors is like a potato: The only good belonging to him is underground."

Sir Thomas Overbury

Find the oldest object
you have in your house.

Draw it, and include either its
actual history or an invented one.

Day 165

"Kind hearts are the gardens,
Kind thoughts are the roots,
Kind words are the flowers,
Kind deeds are the fruits,
Take care of your garden
And keep out the weeds,
Fill it with sunshine
Kind words and kind deeds."
Henry Wadsworth Longfellow

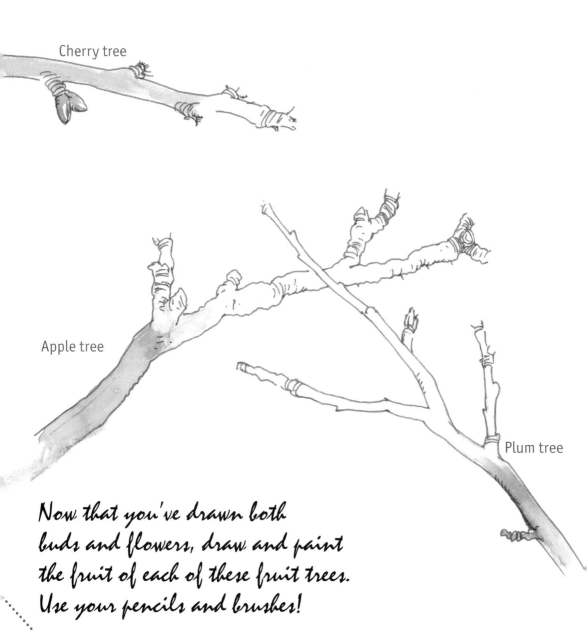

Cherry tree

Apple tree

Plum tree

Now that you've drawn both
buds and flowers, draw and paint
the fruit of each of these fruit trees.
Use your pencils and brushes!

"That proves you are unusual, returned the Scarecrow; and I am convinced the only people worthy of consideration in this world are the unusual ones. For the common folks are like the leaves of a tree, and live and die unnoticed."

L. Frank Baum

The beautiful fruits from yesterday are in danger of being devoured.

Hurry!
Draw a frightening scarecrow.

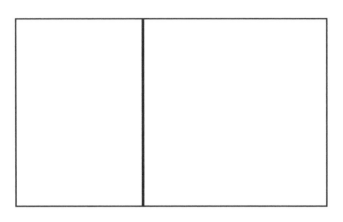

Draw the letter "I" and the letter "J" using fruits, like the "K" on the facing page.

WHO AM I?

At summer's end,
thriving and not
at all ground down,
I wind up ground up.

Answer on Day 210.

Illustrate the riddle below
(after solving it, of course).

The difficulty of this drawing is to personalize
the object in question, without making it so
obvious it gives the answer away.

**WHO
AM
I?**

Despite the drops in my nose,
I don't have a cold.
In fact, I'm so used to them,
I could easily get fitted with a nozzle!

Answer on Day 197.

Day 169

"If the rooster ruffles its feathers, it can easily be plucked."
Burmese proverb

Hey there, rooster . . .

Draw a proud rooster in the barnyard.

"With each egg, the world is new."
Maurice Carême

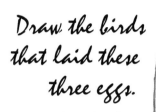

Draw the birds that laid these three eggs.

You can also use your imagination and invent new ones.

Goldcrest

Common Snipe

Mute Swan

Day 171

Find the quill of a goose, hen, or crow, sharpen it, and write a page of text.

If you can't think of anything to say,
write the following phrase ten times:
"I mustn't make mud pies."
If you can't find a quill, use a fountain pen instead.

Sharpening the quill:
Cut the end with a bevel-edged knife,
then sharpen it and make a small slit in
the middle to hold the ink.

*"Reflections on the goose quill: It's as
light as wind and as strong as lightning."*
Victor Hugo

Now you know how to use your quill.

Draw the portrait of a passionate defender of the quill over metallic pens: Victor Hugo.

He wasn't the only one: Chateaubriand and Alfred de Vigny were as well.

Sketched
with a
goose quill

Chateaubriand

Alfred de Vigny

"If a man does not keep pace with his companions, perhaps it is because he hears a different drummer. Let him step to the music which he hears, however measured or far away."

Henry David Thoreau

Can you draw a song?

*"If their father plays the drum,
don't ask why the children dance."*
Algerian proverb

Draw three children
dancing to the
sound of the drum.

*"Life is like a musical instrument; adjust
the tension and it becomes agreeable."*
Demophilus

Drawing a musician isn't easy.
Drawing his hands is even harder!

*Try to draw
the hands of
this guitarist
either from
memory or
using a photograph
or model.*

"I laughed. That's what I call being disarmed."
Alexis Piron

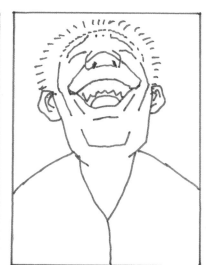

Draw an expression that's somewhere between anger and laughter.

*"A duck's feet are short, that's true, but
stretching them doesn't do any good."*
Zhuang Zi

Draw the following three animals,
exaggerating a part of their body.

"Mouse: an animal which strews its path with fainting women."
Ambrose Bierce

A sketch in four parts.
The plot:

1) A kid is playing with a remote-controlled mouse.
2) He stops in front of the window of a bakery;
3) He throws the mouse in the crowded shop . . .
4) . . . you decide how it ends.

"It's better to be the head of a mouse than the tail of a lion."
Spanish proverb

Combine the head of one animal with the tail or body of another.

Give it a name formulated in the same way,
using two halves of two different names.

"The gift of fantasy has meant more to me than my talent for absorbing positive knowledge."

Albert Einstein

Draw some winged or flying animals that are neither birds nor insects.

Peter, I think they're referring to us!

No, Colin . . . we're not animals!

"Half of one's time must be lost before the other half can be used."
John Locke

Take a moment to
read a comic strip.
Make a note of the most
"talkative" facial expressions.

*On this page, sketch the ones that,
in your opinion, are the most difficult to draw.*

Stick a Post-it to any
drawing featuring
similar expressions.

*"Never fear moving ahead slowly.
Fear only stopping."*

Saying

Day 182

Are you a few drawings behind in your sketchbook?

It's okay, the drawings are probably already
taking shape in your brain. Take stock of your
drawings: Are they too much of one thing, not
enough of another? Is your hand smooth, sharp,
or sloppy? Do your ideas come easily or do you
have to force them? Whatever the case may be,
don't stop now; we have another 183 days to practice!

Tell the remainder of the story.

The parts of the body have their own language.
Try to learn it, in order to make your drawings more expressive.

"Off-screen" is a kind of composition that allows you to guess what isn't being shown.

*"Behold the turtle. He makes progress
only when he sticks his neck out."*
James Bryant Conant

Who would
want to be
a turtle?

Two giant turtles watch
a trailer go by. What
will they say about it?
Illustrate the scene.

"When I was in Africa, I shot an elephant in my pajamas. How he got in my pajamas, I don't know."

Groucho Marx

Groucho Marx was an actor and comedian. "I left nothing to arrive nowhere," he declared.

Have some fun trying to illustrate the quotation above in the style of Groucho Marx: witty and humorous.

"The world is as blue as an orange."
Paul Eluard

Can you illustrate this quote?

If yes, you are a dreamer and free-spirited. If no, you are down-to-earth and realistic.

Draw the
letter *M*
like the
letter *L*
on the
next page.

How strange, this cherry-blue color!

"If the sea was boiling, there would be plenty of cooked fish."
Proverb

*Illustrate this proverb
or invent a new one
that begins with "If . . ."*

If the earth was flat . . .
If mountains were made of rubber . . .

Looks like the sea might have been frozen, not boiling!

Fish: one minute cooking time

"Small streams make large rivers."
Gruter

*Illustrate this drawing
in such a way that the
small streams merge
to create the long river.*

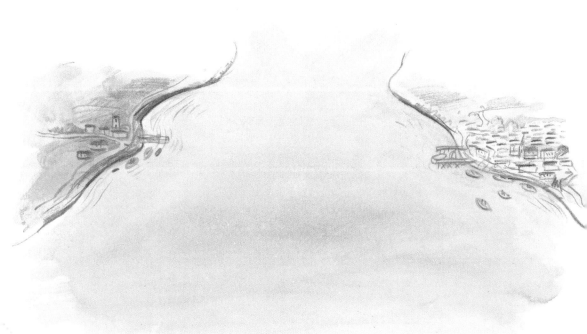

"Throw a lucky man in the river and he will come out with a fish in his mouth."
Arabic proverb

Draw a fisherman with
professional equipment
who isn't catching anything
next to an old man reeling
them in with his homemade
fishing rod.

"When you fish for love, bait with your heart, not your brain."
Mark Twain

Fishing requires the use of bait (like flies);
bait can sometimes be a curious object.

Try to create your own types of bait to catch an animal or person of your choice: in the water, in the air, or on land.

Feel free to make the bait in order to test its usefulness!

Have you ever encountered a mass flight of June bugs on a summer evening? They can sometimes get stuck in your hair.

What a racket! Illustrate a scene in which two children are aghast at a swarm of June bugs.

"Restless thoughts, like a deadly swarm of hornets arm'd, no sooner found alone, but rush upon me thronging."
John Milton

June bug

"My lovely toad,
Why do you weep there?
Because I have the misfortune
Of not being fair."
Robert Desnos

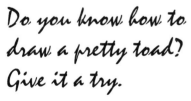

Do you know how to
draw a pretty toad?
Give it a try.

Is it even possible?
Do you have to be a toad to
find another toad beautiful?
Can you put yourself in
a toad's shoes?

Each social group has its own criteria for judging one another.
Do you want to know about another group's criteria?

*Complete this ensemble with
a drawing of your own.*

Which do you like the best?
Which do your friends like best?

Claude Lapointe

Paul Cox

Claude Lapointe

Your drawing

*"Dogs are better than human beings
because they know but do not tell."*
Emily Dickinson

*Give a dog an expression
or gesture of worry,
or any other feeling
of your choice.*

"The originality of an author depends less on his style than on his mode of thought."
Anton Chekhov

Wolf by Éric Gasté

....

Wolf by Granville

....

Wolf by ....

....

Draw your own wolf.
Under each wolf,
write an adjective that best describes it.

Using your left hand,
draw a dog walker and
a dog that resemble each other.

"Beware of secretive men and silent dogs."
Saying

Using your right hand,
draw a dog walker
and a dog that don't
look anything alike.

Answer to the riddle from
Day 168: a watering can.

"A loudmouth doesn't like meeting his match."
Arabic proverb

*Two loudmouths are chatting and
chatting and chatting away . . .*

Imagine that they're discussing
weather, taxes, children . . .
Write their dialogue by superimposing their words and statements,
to the point that it becomes a kind of illegible graffiti . . .

"Those who are absent are assassinated by tongue-lashings."

Paul Scarron

Draw two people sitting at a table talking about a third person who isn't present.

(This can be hinted at by objects: a jacket hanging on the back of a chair, a hat, a chair slightly askew, etc.) The two accomplices are talking behind the absent one's back.

Return to the scene of yesterday.

This time, the third person returns. Imagine the look on the others' faces . . .

"Waist" frame: a composition that captures a person from the waist up in order to accentuate what is being said or done, but without exaggerating it.

"How miserable we would be if we weren't proud of our ancestors."
Laure Conan

Draw a portrait of one of your ancestors
(an ancestor whose photo you have access to,
and which is in good condition).

Try to draw it in your own
style, from the waist up.

*"One is more the product of his time
than the product of his parents."*
African saying

*Draw a person
of today*

(yourself perhaps?)
with the look, attributes,
accessories, and clothes
that go with it.

*Next to him or her,
draw someone
completely opposite,*

who seems at odds with
the style of the day.

*"An artist sees what not longer exists
or what hasn't yet existed in reality."*
Ilya Ehrenburg

Draw an illustrator from the
year 3000 in his or her studio.

Normal Rockwell,
who painted this painting,
often drew in his studio.

"A hero is a man who does what he can. The others don't."
Romain Rolland

Create your very
own superhero
and include his
or her name
and accessories.

(Mask, cape,
weapon, vehicle . . .)

"But, with the slightest reversal of glory, the mask falls, the man remains, and the hero fades away."
Jean-Baptiste Rousseau

The fall of the hero.

Your hero isn't all that gifted. He or she makes blunders.
In the following three boxes, show them to us.

The victim cries out . . .   your hero arrives at the scene . . .   .

It's okay if your hero fails.
He or she still has time to grow.
You can, starting now, begin a long
comic strip showing his or her exploits.

*"Appearances can often
deceive. You can't always
judge by what you see."*
Molière

Two businessmen bow and kiss up to a
person of stature (as evident by his clothing),
but he is actually just a fox in disguise.

"A block of wood toiled over is no longer a block of wood."
Spanish proverb

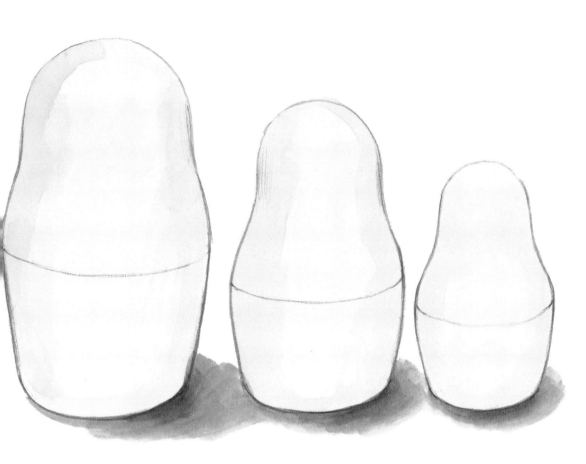

Bring these three Russian dolls to life.

"If I create from the heart, nearly everything works; if from the head, almost nothing."
Marc Chagall

Create a young lady out of scraps of paper.

She is looking in the direction of Polichinelle (the character on the next page).
Frame her using a "thigh shot." (See Day 222.)

*"Polichinelle has a secret
In his saddened heart he keeps it
A deep secret it isn't
This secret of Polichinelle's
You know the truth the secret brings:
His life depends on strings."*

G. Jean

Out of scraps of paper,
create Polichinelle,

who's whispering his secret to
the young lady of yesterday.

"On blue summer evenings,
I shall walk down the pathways,
Getting pricked by wheat ears,
Trampling the short grass."
Arthur Rimbaud

Draw a beautiful
landscape of wheat fields

using watercolors or poster paints.
You might be interested in seeing how Van Gogh drew them.

Answer to the riddle from Day 167: wheat.

*"Wheat mill here
Wheat mill there
If one's in a bind,
The other will grind."*
French saying

John Smith, the miller on Windmill Street,
wants to advertise his goods.

*Design a drawing, acronym, and logo
that he can put on his sacks of wheat.*

*"Tell me what you eat, and
I will tell you who you are."*
Anthelme Brillat-Savarin

Draw three diners in this restaurant
based on what they are eating.

A fancy restaurant. The gentleman is wearing a tuxedo, and the lady is dressed in her evening gown.

They are dining on escargot, artichokes, lobsters, or another plate of your choice that is eaten with the fingers.

"A vacation is like love—anticipated with pleasure, experienced with discomfort, and remembered with nostalgia."

Anonymous

Day 214

Draw your dream vacation destination.

"On holiday at the sea,
In the country of our childhood
In a country worry-free
What shall we do, you and me?
My love, shall we take a stroll along the sea?"

Charles Trenet

Lounging around in the afternoon.

Decorate these three parasols
in styles we've never seen before.

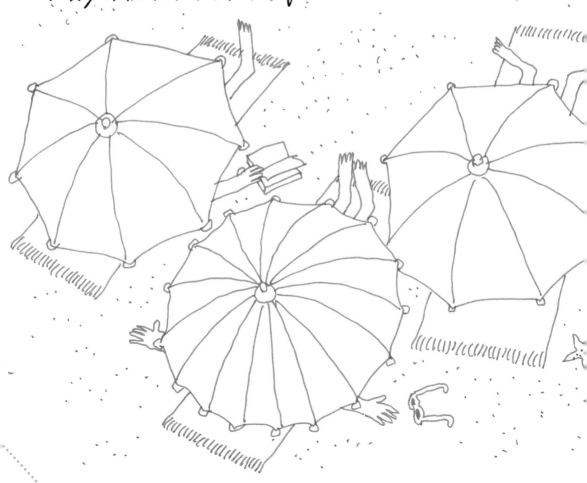

*"Words are written in the sand
I enjoy reading them.
Seeing them wash away doesn't bother me
When the tide recedes, I write them again."*
Jean Dubuffet

Have the child in the drawing write the
letter "N" in the same way as the "O" above.

Try to give it some volume using colored crayons.

"Kites rise highest against the wind, not with it."
Winston Churchill

These kites decorate the sky with spectacular shapes and colors.

Draw and decorate two or three kites

that will make your friends green with jealousy.

*"Each bird sings the praises of the country
where it spent the warm season."*

Fulani proverb

A boy or a girl, still glowing with a tan,
recounts with glee his or her vacation.

Imagine the reactions of his or her friends.

It was awesome . . . the waves, the beach.

It's a pity that only your nose got sun.

Day 219

Draw a face
in the style of
Arcimboldo.

Use objects one normally
finds on the beach
(such as shells, algae,
pieces of wood, etc).

Arcimboldo

Imagine a sailor caught in a raging storm.

*"If you want to go out to sea without the risk
of capsizing, don't buy a boat: Buy an island."*
Marcel Pagnol

Find a good spot in this drawing to hide a treasure chest.

Draw the map leading you to it.

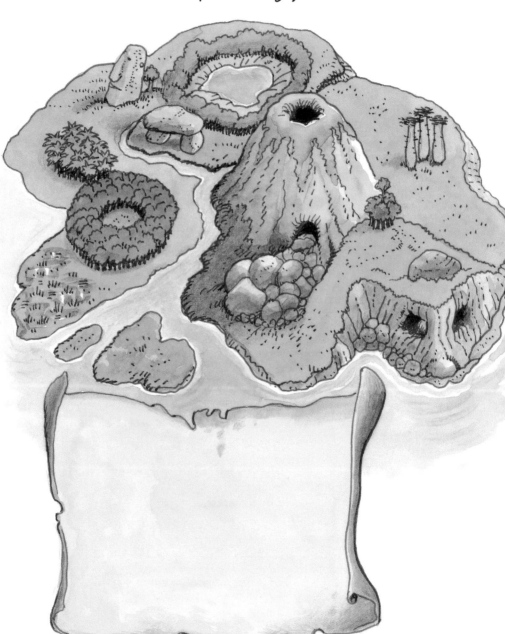

"There's nothing like eavesdropping to show you that the world outside your head is different from the world inside your head."

Thornton Wilder

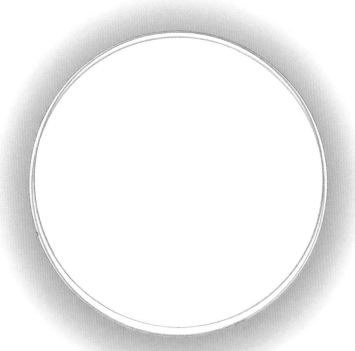

You think you're alone on an island,
but you're actually being watched.

*Draw a "thigh shot" of
the person spying on you
through this eyehole.*

"Thigh shot": People are shown
from mid-thigh up, in order to
accentuate the actions of their
hands and arms. This technique
is often used in Westerns.

Day 223

"Logic is like the sword—those who appeal to it shall perish by it."
Samuel Butler

Draw two pirates crossing swords: Captain Hook and Long John Silver, or two from your imagination.

"Woe to those who approach to listen to their enchanting song, for the flowering meadow where the Sirens are encamped is strewn with a mass of whitened bones and human debris. Don't stop, Odysseus!"

Homer, from *The Odyssey*

Draw a beautiful, enchanting siren.

Day 225

Draw the Chimera: a vision far from that of the beauty of the siren.

The Chimera is a fire-breathing female monster with a lion's head, a goat's body, and a dragon's tail.

We have the right to demand royalties from the Chimera.

"The spendthrift robs his heirs; the miser robs himself."
Jean de la Bruyère

At least
I won't
get mugged!

*Illustrate a miser
clinging to his change purse.*

Draw him in the surroundings and the clothing style of today.

"Humor is the ability to see three sides to one coin."
Ned Rorem

Draw a set of coins in your own image.

Head

Tail

"Love is the only passion that pays for itself in a currency of its own fabrication."
Stendhal

Draw your own money.

Note the amounts that you would like to possess.

"He said he was like a crocodile. You never knew whether he was trying to smile or preparing to swallow you up."

Winston Churchill

Humorous drawing.

Have some fun with the crocodile in the above quotation.

Transform him into a shoe, a bag, or anything else . . .

I told her, "You have beautiful crocodile skin, you know," and then WHAM! . . . But . . . I was only talking about her bag!

"A camel doesn't consider its hump a defect."
Algerian proverb

Day 230

Draw a camel traveling the desert as part of a caravan.

"Elephants are always drawn smaller than life, but fleas larger."

Jonathan Swift

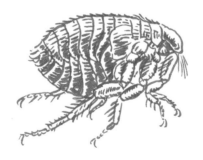

A question of scale

What can you place next to the elephant to
show how big it is in real life? What can you place next to the
flea so that one can see how small it is in real life?

"Since the invention of the phonogram and the gramophone, the parrot has become an unnecessary creature."

Alphonse Allais

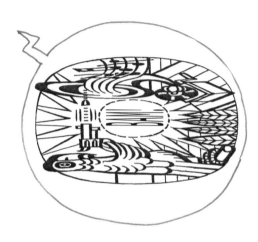

For fun, draw a parrot with beautiful feathers.

What is it saying to you
in its own language?
Is it difficult to understand?
You will soon decode it:
See Day 239.

Day 233

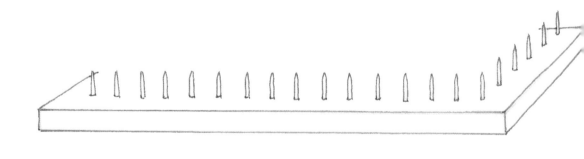

Draw a fakir
playing the flute
that makes the snake
on the next page dance.

*"The snake shrugs its shoulders
when you walk on its feet."*
Stéphane Collaro

The snake writhes out of the basket.

Draw a cobra or a snake of your own invention.

Day 235

Draw all the different ways imaginable to get from the country of palm trees to the country of pine trees.

"For my part, I travel not to go anywhere, but to go: I travel for travel's sake."
Robert Louis Stevenson

Draw a person at the end of a very long walk through the desert.

A walk? What exactly do you mean by that?

Decorate the skateboards below.

Show it to a true skateboard fanatic.
What does he or she think of it?

Draw your mailman from memory.

Take a good look at him next time he delivers your mail and see whether or not your visual memory was correct.

Air mail?

*"Anonymous letters have the
advantage of not requiring a
response."*
Alexandre Dumas

Write a hidden message

in two words or two very short sentences,
stretching out the letters so as to make them almost illegible.

Egyptian is a font that
might help you in creating
your coded message.

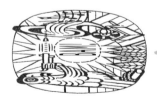

The parrot's message
is a drawing that must
be read directly in front
of you, at eye-level.

Day 240

"Send me a postcard! Send me the night's starry sky, the deep craters of Vesuvius!"

Pacere Titinga

A letter needs a stamp to reach its destination. Have you ever participated in a stamp-making contest? If yes, paste your project to this page.

Or create a stamp that you would like to send on an envelope.

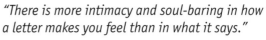

Day 241

On this page, paste the most unique envelope you have ever received.

If you don't have one, have your friends
compete to see who can write to you in style.

Now it's your turn to make a beautiful drawing on an envelope!

You can copy one you've already received (why not send it and start a collection?).
Drawing on an envelope constitutes something called mail art:
Some artists depend on the mail system for their creativity.

As Ray Johnson says:
"Mail art belongs to everyone;
it is for everyone who sees it,
not just the person who receives it."

What if this is worth a fortune?!

Day 243

"Paper speaks when people stop talking."
French saying

Say nothing   See nothing   Hear nothing

*Continue the drawing of
the three wise monkeys.*

Complete the following table. Have we made any progress between yesterday and today?

Yesterday   Today

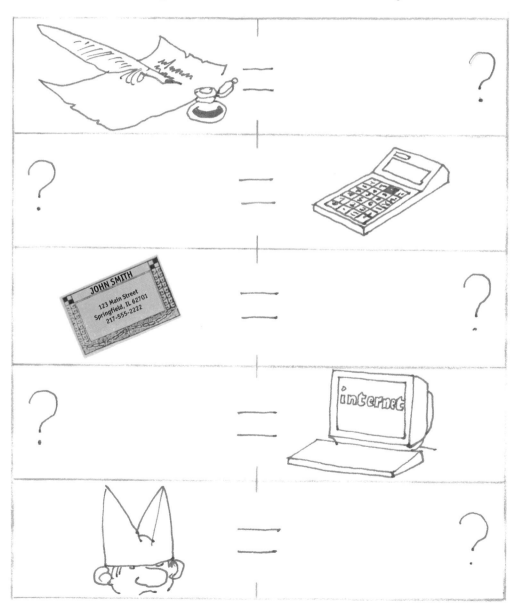

Try to bring some nuance into your drawings.
Draw six completely different apples.

Green apple	Yellow apple	Appetizing apple
Spotted apple	Rotten apple	Apple core

"Adam and Eve were punished for being vegetarians. They should have eaten the snake."

Robert Sabatier

Draw Adam and Eve looking perplexed before the snake.

"The apple never falls far from the tree."
Saying

Wrap the tempting
snake around the
branch of this tree.

Day 248

*"Love is like a poisonous mushroom—you don't
know if it is the real thing until it is too late."*

Anonymous

*Draw two beautiful close-ups
of edible mushrooms.*

"Don't think of the vessel itself, but of its contents."
Talmud

And now draw two beautiful,
poisonous mushrooms.

"Man is the cruelest animal."
Friedrich Nietzsche

Photomontages can sometimes
produce surprising effects.

*Paste some human faces
on a photograph depicting
a group of animals.*

Who looks worse?

"Every time a child says:
'I don't believe in fairies,'
there is a fairy somewhere
that falls down dead."
J. M. Barrie, from *Peter Pan*

But fairies haven't completely disappeared!

Imagine a fairy in the city and a fairy in the country;
vary the details of their magic wands accordingly.

"To better see other people's defects, one uses a magnifying glass; when it comes to his own, he covers his eyes."
Paul Chrétien-Audruger

Draw a portrait of Miss Melusine, a very demanding client.

"As harmless as a word might seem to he who spoke it, it is as hurtful to he who hears it."
Spanish proverb

Make the most of your drawing experience:
Now draw a caricature of Melusine.

Day 254

Melusine saw the caricature you made of her.
She is furious and has put a curse on you.
You have no choice but to redraw her portrait and improve it, but now you have the added handicap of having to wear mittens or gloves!

"You can't explain anything to a child; you must bewitch him."
Marina Tsvetaeva

Draw an "ex-voto" depicting a vow being fulfilled,

such as the curse that Melusine put on you.

"Ex-voto": a painting or object suspended in a venerated place, in the aftermath of a fulfilled vow.

Day 256

"Words are like a spider web: They are a shelter for the wise and a trap for the foolish."

Malagasy proverb

A spider web as illustrated by the *Petit Larousse* (a French dictionary)

Draw a spider web suspended in these branches.

Draw the spider web again.

"I don't write poetry, I simply expose what exists. I don't have any preconceived notions. I react to the topography of a place, the light, the climate and materials."

Nils Udo

To change its function, color in each surface of the web: you've just transformed a trap into an abstract work of art!

"Habits start off like threads of silk and quickly become cables of steel."

Spanish saying

Draw two people playing with (real) bits of string,

like the two people at the bottom of this page.

"One regrets the loss even of one's worst habits; perhaps one regrets them the most."

Oscar Wilde

You must have developed some drawing habits by now: a certain way of drawing hair, hands, eyes, the nose . . .

On this page, you might want to try changing some of your drawing habits, either by giving them up or by strengthening them!

"The moment one gives close attention to anything, even a blade of grass, it becomes a mysterious, awesome, indescribably magnificent world in itself."

Henry Miller

An image is composed of a series of fields, such as the foreground and the background. Sometimes, these fields can be superimposed in interesting ways, creating something entirely new. If they're used constructively, they can become the whole purpose of the scene!

Play with this idea: Create two images containing a foreground and background that interfere with each other.

*Draw something
surprising coming out of
the magician's hat.*

*"Chasing after shadows
Many people blunder;
So numerous are they
One cannot count the number."*

Jean de La Fontaine

*Using black ink,
sketch some shadows
with a paintbrush.*

*"Seated in the shadow of a rock
I see the shadow of a coachman
Holding the shadow of a brush,
Cleaning the shadow of a horse-drawn carriage."*
Les frères Perrault

Day 263

Illustrate the quotation of the day using shadow puppets.

Shadow theater involves figures and objects
casting their shadow on a screen lit from behind.

"I have often thought it would be a blessing if each human being were stricken blind and deaf for a few days during their early adult life. Darkness would make them more appreciative of sight; silence would teach them the joys of sound."

Helen Keller

Using black paper, cut out the profile of a person's face. Even better, get someone you know to sit for you, and use their face as a model.

Silhouettes cut out of black paper were very much in vogue in the eighteenth century. On the left is a silhouette-painter's chair. Next to that, the person sitting down is Voltaire (by Jean Huber).

*"When the eyebrows grow,
the worries begin."*
Jules Renard

Day 265

*Complete this face by pasting on thread for
the eyelashes, fur for the beard, grass for the hair,
and two plastic circles for eyeglasses . . .*

"An ideal man searching for an ideal woman? This is the best way to stay single."

Dominique Blondeau

Draw the letter *P* like the *Q* on the next page, by contorting a person's body.

Male, 32 years old, available, 5 ft 8 in, 165 lbs, light brown hair, blue eyes, average-looking, very handy, loves to travel and seeks companionship with Female, 32–40 years old, single or widowed, kind, faithful, wanting children, and searching for a life based on mutual understanding and harmony.

Want ads can be seen as a source of subjects worth illustrating.

Imagine the person who placed this ad; draw him, as well as the woman he hopes to meet.

"An ideal husband is one who comes home early, does the shopping, washes the dishes and looks after the kids. Conclusion: An ideal husband is a wife!"

Bruno Gaccio

Female, 45 years old, single, red-headed, sweet, adorable, social, kind, affectionate, loves animals both large and small, mushrooms, and long walks in the forest, searching for Male, 42–52 years old, single, secure, honest, who enjoys long walks, chocolate, and living life in harmony with another.

Like yesterday, draw a portrait of the person who placed this ad next to her ideal companion.

*"Speak when you are angry—and you'll make
the best speech you'll ever regret."*

Dr. Laurence J. Peter

Draw two people shouting at each other.

Communicate their feelings by way of the shape of your
word balloons and the size and punctuation used in the text.

"One cannot read if he doesn't know the letters; letters are only erased by meaning."
Alain (Emile Chartier)

Create a head or profile using only letters, numbers, and punctuation marks.

"The person who doesn't know where his next dollar is coming from usually doesn't know where his last dollar went."

Anonymous

You must know the dollar sign fairly well by now.

Incorporate it in your drawings as a figurative element wherever it fits.

$ $ $ $$$ $$ $ $$ $ $$ $ $$ $ $$

"Life is like a cash register, in that every account, every thought, every deed, like every sale, is registered and recorded."

Fulton J. Sheen

Incorporate some coins into your drawings wherever they fit. Use your imagination!

"Even if your pockets are empty, keep your hat on straight."
Spanish proverb

Two men prepare for a duel.
This page features a hero from a Western.

*Finish drawing his face
and place a cowboy hat on
his head. Don't forget the
shadow it casts over his face.*

"A flatterer is nothing more than an odious and treacherous animal."
Jacques Bénigne Bossuet

This page shows the treacherous, deceitful card player.

Finish his face and fit him with his derby hat.

"To fly in the wind: This is the goal of a fallen leaf."
Gustave Thibon

The card player is exposed!
He leaves the town in a hurry,
leaving a cloud of cash in his wake.

*Draw a crowd running around,
grasping and fighting over the money.*

*"The long sobs
of the violins
of autumn
wound my heart
with languorous monotones."*
Paul Verlaine

*Imagine an autumn
landscape through this window.*

Feel free to experiment with abstract,
warm, or muted colors.

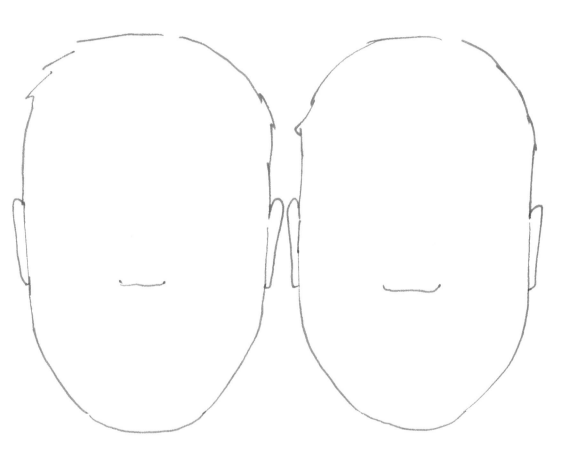

"Never confuse sadness with boredom."
Jules Renard

You're not someone who confuses sadness with boredom!

Draw the two emotions on the faces above.
Make sure you bring out the nuances of the two.

"The fuzzy contours of the peach,
The amber hues of the golden grape,
The frosty sugar of the plum."
Edmond and Jules de Goncourt

Place two or three real or
imaginary fruits on the fruit plate.
Try to make them as appetizing as possible.

"Don't judge each day by the harvest you reap but by the seeds that you plant. "
Robert Louis Stevenson

Day 278

*Continue this drawing of grapevines.
Using watercolors, paint it in autumnal hues.*

Day 279

"The wine urges me on, the bewitching wine, which sets even a wise man to singing and to laughing gently, and rouses him up to dance and brings forth words which were better unspoken."

Homer

Create an outrageous costume for Bacchus to wear onstage.

Bacchus is the Roman god of the vine and wine, also known as Dionysus in Greek mythology. His worshippers contributed to the development of tragedy and lyrical art.

*"Tragedy is the collaboration between
a double-edged sword and a razor."*
Miguel Zamacoïs

*A couple of TV viewers and their dog
watch a very, very long and complicated show.*

"Nowadays, man walks one-armed and muzzled through a palace of mirages."
Michel Tournier

Following the model, create a trompe l'oeil column.

As indicated in the diagram, curl a strip of paper and connect the two ends together. Paint one side of it yellow, and the other side blue . . . What happened? You just discovered one of the properties of the Möbius strip (Möbius was a German mathematician, 1790–1868).

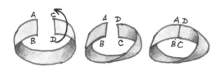

"Stairs can either go up or down, depending on the direction in which one takes them."

Jean Ferrat

Draw an architectural impossibility, playing with optical illusions, like the never-ending staircase to the right.

Consult M. C. Escher's work, trompe l'oeils, or optical illusions . . .

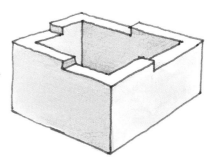

"Underwear is to vaudeville as the toga is to tragedy."
Carlo Rim

In this classic painting,
"The Rape of the Sabine Women,"
draw in a person for fun—
a person who doesn't belong.

The intruder will either be visible right away,
or, with the right technique, will only be
detectable by examining the painting up close.

*"A good reputation stays put;
a bad one runs in the streets."*
Russian proverb

*Two wicked
gossips criticize
a passerby.*

Draw two people in
the foreground and
the passerby in
the background.

"His bark is worse than his bite."
Western proverb

*Draw the animals corresponding
to their word balloons.*

"Don't burden your thoughts with the weight of your shoes."
André Breton

Draw a person walking. In the first box, his strides are light; in the second box, his steps are heavy and leaden.

"Everything is a miracle. It is a miracle that one does not dissolve in one's bath like a lump of sugar."
Pablo Picasso

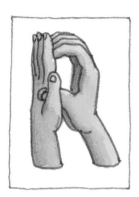

Draw a sugar cube; try to draw it as accurately as possible, so that if someone were to see it, they would say, "That's a sugar cube!"

(And not a sponge or a brick . . .) This type of drawing constitutes one of many small traps of representation. Be careful!

"It is possible to make jam from dreams. Just add fruit and sugar."
Stanislaw Jerzy Lec

Draw the letter *S* like the letter *R* from Day 287, with two hands forming the letter.

AESOP'S FABLES

THE FOX AND THE RAVEN

erstein

Make a drawing for glycophiles.

What? You don't know what a glycophile is?

Well, it's someone who collects sugar packets.

Draw one or two wrappers that could be included in a collection of sugar packets.

"What good the mouth has is a gift from the tongue."
African proverb

. **Hébreu :** בוקר טוב

. **Arabe :** صباح الخير

. **Indien :** नमस्कार *(to several persons)*

. **Russe :** доброе утро

Here is a sampling of polite people greeting each other in their own language.

Once you figure out their nationality, draw them in next to their word balloons.

You can use traditional clothing, or put in an object

or detail that gives away their country of origin.

"People shape language. They make it colorful and light, lively and sonorous. If the erudite shaped it, it would be muffled and heavy."

Anatole France

> IAY AVEHAY
> ISCOVEREDDAY ETHAY
> EANINGMAY OFAY IFELAY.

> ONAY, OUYAY
> AVENTHAY. IAY AVEHAY
> ISCOVEREDDAY ETHAY
> EANINGMAY OFAY
> IFELAY!

Draw two extremely erudite scholars exchanging extremely learned thoughts.

Do you know how to speak like them?

"It's okay to know nothing; after all, one can always learn."
Saying

Tom Sawyer

It's exam time.
Relive this frantic
(or memorable) moment.

"If I were the headmaster of a school, I would get rid of the history teacher and get a chocolate teacher instead; at least my students would study a subject that affects them all."

Roald Dahl

Caricatures.
The physical features
and tics of some of your
old teachers have surely
marked you over the years.
Share them with us!

Who is it supposed
to be, anyway?

What do
you think?

Day 293

"When you start with a portrait and try to find pure form by abstracting more and more, you must end up with an egg."
Pablo Picasso

If you draw a cubist portrait, what natural laws will you break?

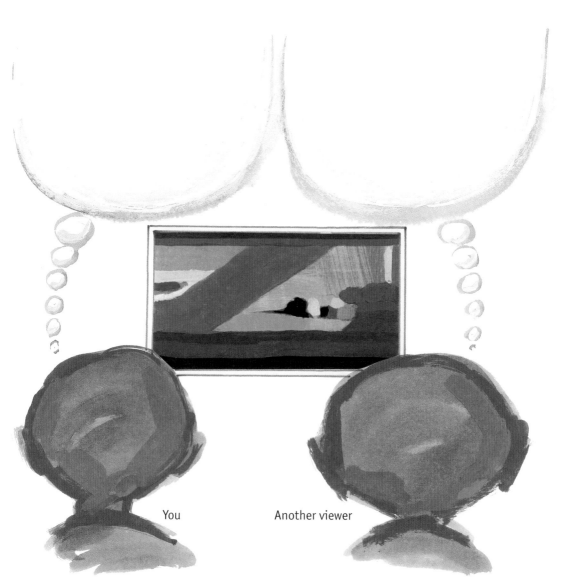

You   Another viewer

*In your word balloon, draw or write what
this painting means to you, if anything.*

Hide your balloon and ask another viewer to do the same.
Compare your impressions . . .

*"Transformation is to be feared
in all instances, except the bad."*
Michel de Montaigne

*In two drawings, slowly transform
this broom and stool into a giraffe.*

You're now ready to make an animated drawing.

Use camouflage to make the first person
"disappear" into the jungle. Now do the reverse:
make the second person stand out even
more in his surroundings.

"Out of the crooked timber of humanity no straight thing was ever made."

Immanuel Kant

Equipped with only a ruler and compass, draw a lively, animated figure.

A trick: Draw different parts of the figure on separate scraps of paper. Before completing your final drawing, play with the various shapes and try to figure out which combination allows for the most movement.

"Found art": collecting objects of every kind in order to strip them of their primary function and transform them into works of art.

Using a copper or iron wire, or any other found objects or materials, create a figure of a little man.

Feel free to create it on a separate sheet of paper, as the materials you're using may be hefty. Paste a copy of it here and create a separate file containing all the drawings that don't fit in this workbook.

Image by Christian Voltz.

*"Millions of men have lived to fight, build palaces and boundar,
shape destinies and societies; but the compelling force of all ti,
has been the force of originality and creation profoundly affect,
the roots of human spirit."*

Ansel Ad

*Action is hard
to illustrate.*

Draw someone playing a sport,
running away, or dancing.

PLOC

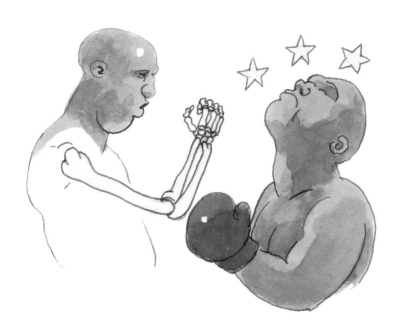

A nice uppercut!
On three superimposed sketches, draw the arm's bones covered by muscles, then skin, then the glove.

If you're not in the mood for an anatomy lesson, invent some muscles (after all, once they're covered, you'll no longer see them!).

"When memory goes looking for firewood, it brings back whatever bundle it likes best."
Birago Diop

Draw the first classmate that pops into your head.

Now ask yourself:
Why him, or why her?
Is he or she the best-
looking in your class?
The easiest to draw?
The most "something"?

In the style of riddle drawings, hide several objects in either an interior or exterior setting.

Make a legend of the objects to find.

The objects must be recognizable, but they don't necessarily have to go with the setting they're in, and they can be drawn sideways or upside down.

Find what I hid in this drawing!

"The potter drinks from a broken jug."
Persian saying

Bring this saying to life: Choose a profession and illustrate it.

Suggestions: plumber,

mechanic, doctor . . .

Ask someone to do a drawing you've never tried before, or one you haven't had much success with. Or invent another exercise.

It lacks emotion!

"Fashions fade, style is eternal."
Yves Saint Laurent

Make your mark (on this page)!

Draw yourself in your finest clothing—the coolest you own—or your favorite outfit.

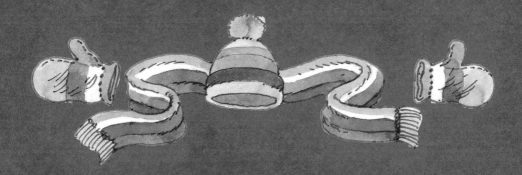

"There is almost nothing that has such a keen sense of fun as a fallen leaf."

J. M. Barrie

Transform two autumn leaves into characters.

Have them act out a scene or a little sketch: a story of leaves.

Draw the letter *U* and *V* in foliage, like the letter *T* on the previous page.

"When life is a forest,
Each day is a tree.
When life is a tree,
Each day is a branch.
When life is a branch,
Each day is a leaf."

Jacques Prévert

Paste a beautiful autumn leaf to this page.

Note where you found the leaf and what kind of tree it came from.

Draw a close-up of it, if you feel like it.

How much should I cut for you?

"The naked truth is always better than the best-dressed lie."
Ann Landers

*Better put clothes on these people
before they realize they forgot to!*

"Winter fought off every last flowering.
Barren trees dot the horizon.
Now there are only white skeletons and ghosts."
Guy de Maupassant

Day 309

Sketch some of these tree shadows
that resemble humans or animals.

"The least one can do for someone lost in the fog is to show him the direction of the light."
Vincent Ravalec

Draw the fog surrounding the boat and the light of a lighthouse piercing the grayness.

"From birth, we live among ghosts; not only those who frighten us, but also those who are good advisors, both funny and amiable."

Alfred Kubin

Do you know a ghost like the ones described by Kubin? We would be happy to make its acquaintance.

"Words sometimes serve as a smoke screen to obscure the truth, rather than as a searchlight to reveal it."
Anonymous

It's chilly outside. Smoke is coming out of all the chimneys.

Draw each cloud of smoke using a different technique.

(Pencil, watercolors, poster paint, quill pen, felt-tip marker, etc . . .)

*"I like watching the streetlamps gleam in the distance.
It's a night concert. It's the big city . . ."*

Alphonse Esquiros

Draw this couple's shadows against the wall.

See Day 315.

"Does adventure await on the corner of the street?"
Jacques Dutronc

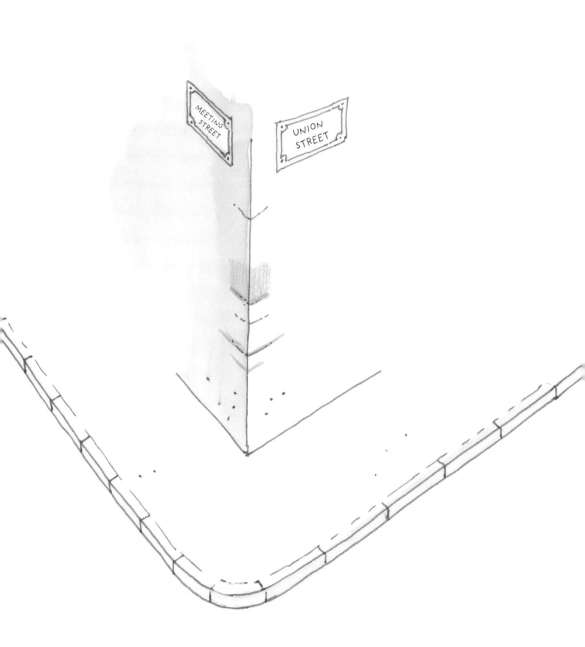

Draw two people approaching the corner from both sides of the sidewalk, (or a person and an animal) whose encounter is bound to be either spectacular or catastrophic.

"Sometimes you catch yourself walking on the very edge of a sidewalk like you did when you were a kid, as though the border was the only thing that mattered, the edge of the world."

Philippe Delerm

What kinds of things have you done on the sidewalks of your neighborhood, in your hometown? Think of an activity you remember and draw it.

The solution from Day 313.

"The real voyage of discovery consists not in seeking new landscapes, but in having new eyes."

Marcel Proust

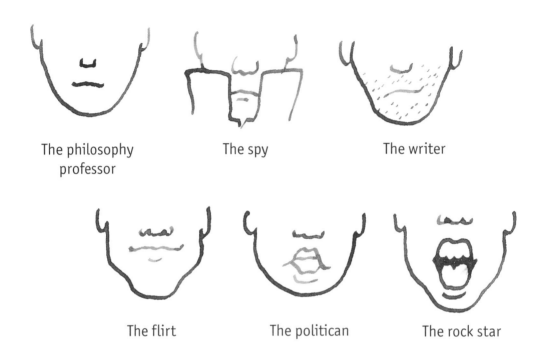

The philosophy professor

The spy

The writer

The flirt

The politican

The rock star

The crazy scholar

Miss World

The American tourist

Draw the glasses through which these characters see the world.

Orient the following faces toward the designated targets.

Be precise.

Ken

Liselotte

b)

a)

Emma

c)

Zoé

d)

A) Ken is looking at the flea.
B) Liselotte watches the spider's every move.
C) Emma keeps an eye on the grasshopper.
D) Zoé peers at the fly.

Day 318

"In a spacious armchair, the blessed hearth so near,
Through the winter—to infinity! I shall stay here."
Hippolyte Laroche

Make two or three
sketches of a dreamer
lounging in his
armchair.

To each
his own!

"A television set is a fair where people come to see the wonders of the world."
Kazimierz Brandys

It's a riot!

Draw a row of politicians.

Use photographs or caricatures to help you in your drawing.

Day 320

Draw the most frightening dragon you can imagine.
Don't hesitate to use both pages for your drawing.

"Fairies do their washing in a soap bubble and make their soup in a will-o'-the-wisp."

Béatrix Beck

In a corner of the page not occupied by your dragon, draw the fairy as described in the quotation above.

Day 322

"When day turns to night,
Under the leaves we dance
In the simple clarity of the moon's light,
A thousand nude nymphs in trance
Through the bushes the enamored faun follow suit."

Jean-François Sarasin

Illustrate the dance of the nymphs
under the bluish light of the moon.

Draw the number 18 like the 17 on the previous page, using tree trunks.

Fauns: deities in human form, but with horns and goat's hooves.

Nymphs: female deities; goddesses of the water, woods, and mountains who personify the bounty of nature.

Illustrate a faun interested in the scene next door.

Day 324

Draw an animal walking through the snow—make it white, against a black background (the sky).

*"Sunshine cannot bleach the snow,
Nor time unmake what poets know."*
Ralph Waldo Emerson

Gray in gradation.

These trees are aligned from darkest to lightest.

*Create a gradation of the color gray,
represented here by size.*

Now do the reverse: The smallest house is the darkest and the biggest house is
the lightest. What effect does this have?

The more a color shifts, especially in autumn,
the weaker it is and the more it gives off a gray-blue hue.

"Take, if you must, this little bag of dreams,
Unloose the cord, and they will wrap you round."
William Butler Yeats

Draw every bag you know:

Knapsack
Bag of tricks
Fleabag
Bag of bones
Backpack
A bag that holds everything . . .

"We are easily moved by things we don't normally see and not enough by what we see every day."
Comtesse de Genlis

Empty your bag or pockets.
Draw all the objects you find in them.

"If wise men were hairs the world would need a wig."
Anonymous

Play the role of a hairdresser.
Draw one or two extravagant hairstyles.

Proposed covers for the book
Pierre l'Ébouriffé (*Slovenly Peter*)

"Femininity in a man is like sugar in whisky. Masculinity in a woman is like yeast in bread. Without these ingredients, the result is flat, lacking spice and flavor."

Edna Ferber

Choose two passport photos:
one of a man, and the other of a woman.

As skillfully as possible, transform the man into a woman and the woman into a man.

Compose a family:

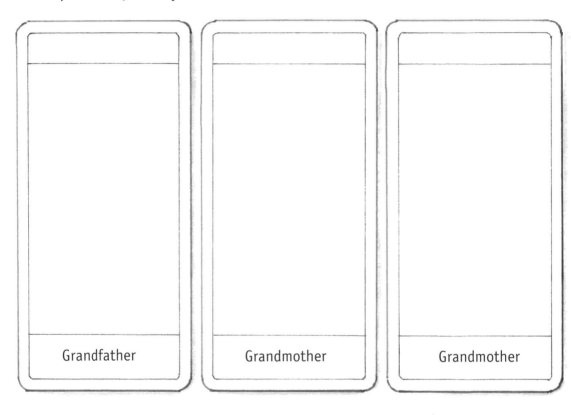

| Grandfather | Grandmother | Grandmother |

"When I was kidnapped, my parents snapped into action: They rented out my room."
Woody Allen

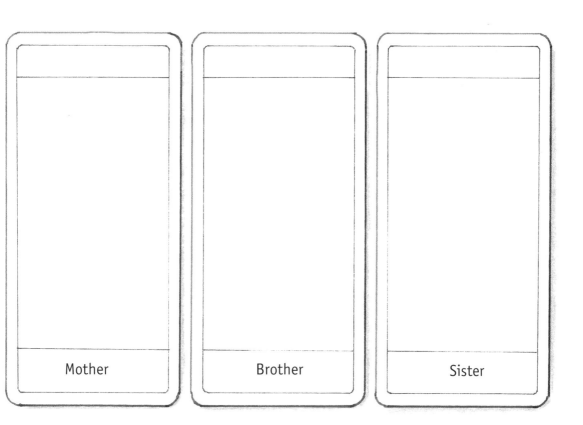

Mother

Brother

Sister

"The lives of most men are patchwork quilts. Or at best one matching outfit with a closet and laundry bag full of incongruous accumulations."

Jesse Owens

Create a character using scraps of material (you can either sew or glue them together).

"We don't choose our parents, we don't choose our family
Nor do we choose the sidewalks of Manila,
Paris, or Algiers to learn how to walk."

Maxime Le Forestier

Draw a shop window in which all
kinds of parents are for sale.

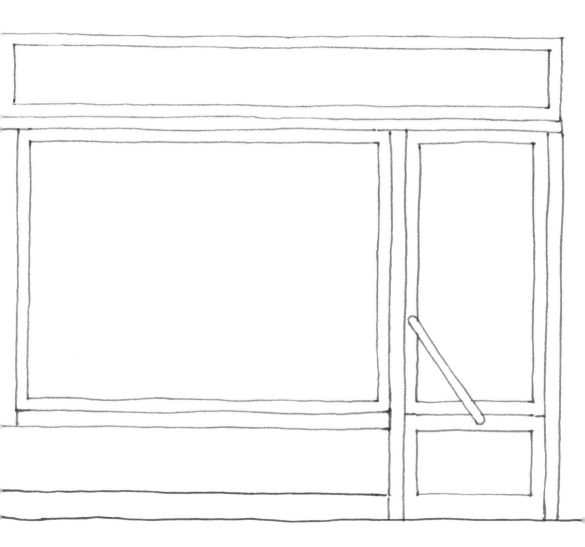

"Parents were invented to make children happy by giving them something to ignore."

Ogden Nash

Can you draw your parents?
(Or a couple of your choice . . .)

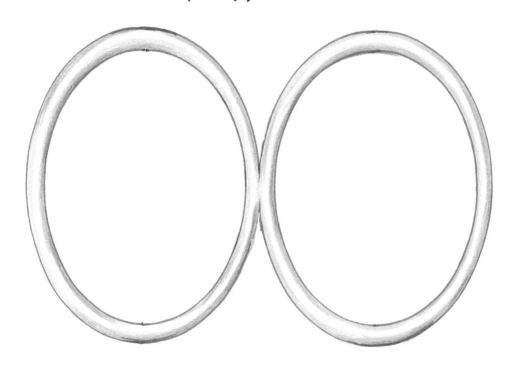

"I have loads of new and brilliant ideas,
But the brilliant ones aren't new
And the new ones aren't brilliant."
Marcel Achard

Draw yourself at the height of success.

Or the moment you've always dreamed of:
Winning the World Series,
being voted president,
becoming a rock star, or
even becoming a famous illustrator . . .

"Fear has its use but cowardice has none."
Mahatma Gandhi

Do you remember the last time you experienced true fear?
Can you re-create the moment here?

"A human being is an ingenious assembly of portable plumbing."
Christopher Morley

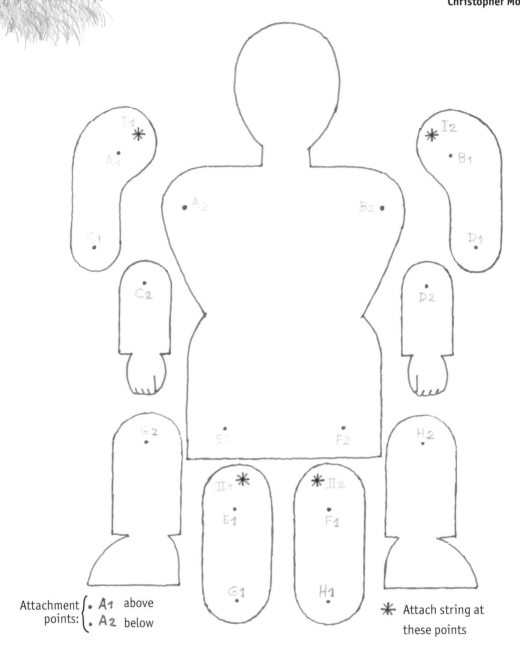

Attachment points:
{ • **A1** above
{ • **A2** below

✻ Attach string at these points

Construct a puppet.
Draw the model (preferably larger than it appears here) and then make it using cardboard.

Collages.

Look through some magazines and catalogs and cut out any noses, eyes, and mouths you see. Now mix them together to create some interesting faces.

Your teeth are so big!

The better to bite you with!

"There are hundreds of languages in the world, but a smile speaks them all."

Anonymous

You are in a foreign country where you don't speak the language, looking for a restaurant, hotel, or some other destination.

Draw the gestures you'll need to make so that others will understand you.

"One hand washes the other."
Saying

It's not easy to draw hands in action.

Try to draw some difficult hand movements: using scissors, knitting, or any other movements you can think of.

*"Sometimes you have to put
your foot down to get a leg up."*
David Weinbaum

We rarely draw bare feet.

*Draw a foot in
your own style.*

Which style does it come

closest to?

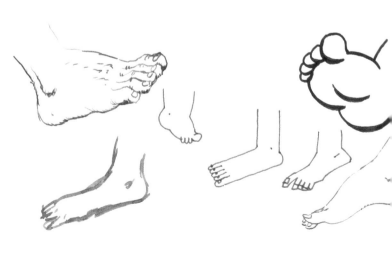

"My right foot is jealous of my left foot.
When one takes a step, the other wants to overtake it
And I, the imbecile that I am, simply walk."

Raymond Devos

Draw the letters *X*, *Y*, and *Z* in the style of the *W* on the previous page.

Draw a race:

One runner jogs, another dashes ahead, and a third stumbles behind . . .

"To truly appreciate a country, one must eat it, drink it, and listen to it sing."

Michel Déon

Figure out the native country of the musician sitting at the table (it's easy!).

Draw his partner sitting in front of him:

He comes from a country recognizable by his

choice of musical instrument, food, and drink.

"A kiss is to love as a thermometer is to medicine. Without it, you would never fully grasp the magnitude of your condition."

Pierre Daninos

Draw several warm ways of greeting someone

(in your town or neighborhood, between butterflies, cannibals, etc . . .)

BAM!

"A couple is the joining together of two mismatched people."

Adrien Decourcelle

Draw two couples on a park bench
who don't seem to go together.

"Beware of couples who hold hands. They hold hands because they're afraid if they let go, they'll kill each other."

Groucho Marx

Complete these drawings in your own style.

"We can't be held responsible for the craziness in our brains. We can chase away immoral and illogical thoughts, but we can't prevent them from forming."

Jules Renard

You're an illustrator, and you're tasked with illustrating the four scenes in this scenario.

Draw them in pencil first.

A man is sitting on a bench reading the newspaper.

An ostrich sits down next to him. The man looks at it, surprised. "What?" asks the ostrich.

After sketching them in pencil, complete the final

"It takes true courage to be a dove, but no honor to be an ostrich."

Anonymous

Man: "I'm astonished—
flabbergasted!"
Ostrich: "Oh really? Why?"

Man: "Because . . . you look
exactly like my brother!"

drawings with the dialogue in word balloons.

"Perhaps people are allowed to visit the zoo in order to entertain the animals."

André Birabeau

It's Sunday. A family of animals marches past the cage of an endangered species, *Homo sapiens sapiens*.

Draw this Sunday scene.

"What if we made stuffed children toys for bears?"
Patrick Sébastien

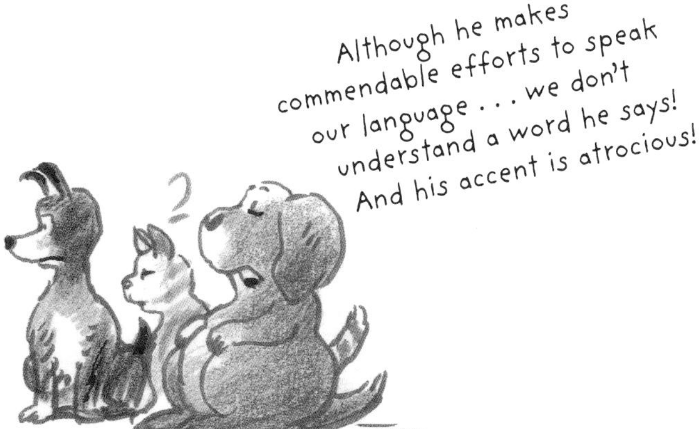
Although he makes commendable efforts to speak our language . . . we don't understand a word he says! And his accent is atrocious!

A cub plays with a toy Superman (or another hero or heroine of your choice).

"Things take on the color of our upsets."
André Birabeau

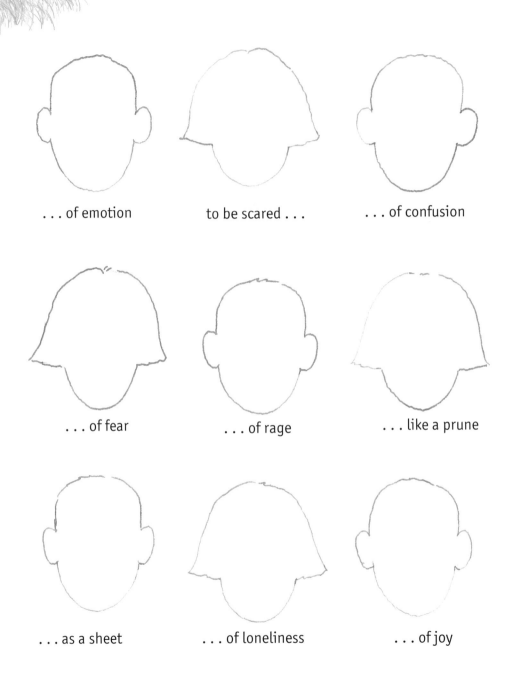

. . . of emotion

to be scared . . .

. . . of confusion

. . . of fear

. . . of rage

. . . like a prune

. . . as a sheet

. . . of loneliness

. . . of joy

*It's your turn to color in the faces
and finish the descriptions.*

*"Attitude is the mind's paintbrush.
It can color any situation."*
Alexander Lockhart

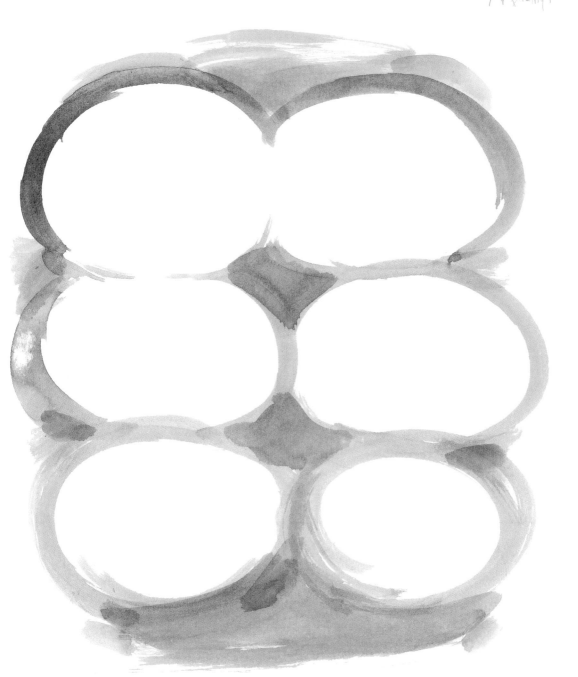

Draw these different ambiances using color:
A glacial ambiance, a warm ambiance, an electric ambiance,
a dramatic ambiance, and two other ambiances of your choice . . .

"Telephone: an invention of the devil which abrogates some of the advantages of making a disagreeable person keep his distance."

Ambrose Bierce

Observe some cell phone users talking in the street.

Draw some of their gestures and expressions.

That doesn't seem very practical!

"I think that if you think that I'm thinking what you're thinking, we just might understand each other."

Jean Duvivier

Day 354

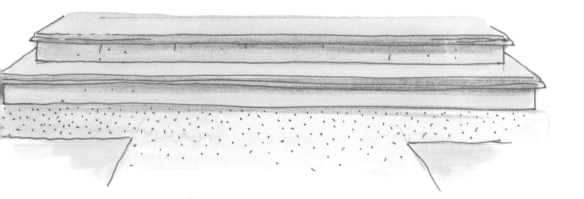

Three politicians are congratulating one another publicly on these steps after conducting a crucial meeting.

Hint at some signs of discord behind their facade of harmony and understanding.

"An opera singer is the type of person who gets stabbed in the back and who, rather than bleeds, starts to sing."

Judy Canova

Paint the portrait of a female singer you admire, or one you'd rather run from.

"Later I would like to be a conductor, a trapeze artist, or a music-hall artist; anything but an adult."

François Morel

The conductor is in a trance. He's waving four, six, eight arms at once.

Draw him as he appears from behind.

prestissimo

"When an oak tree smells of fir,
it knows the end is near."
Raymond Devos

Form and matter.

Draw the
shape of
a fir tree
but with
oak leaves.

That way, it looks
like a fir tree from
afar, but up close,
it's a funny-looking
oak tree! Think of
other objects that
can be used in this
game.

"Is it so small a thing
To have enjoy'd the sun,
To have lived light in the spring,
To have loved, to have thought, to have done . . ."
Matthew Arnold

Each of these suns tell a story or a memory.

Make them shine brightly!

"It is only by drawing often, drawing everything, drawing incessantly, that one fine day you discover to your surprise that you have rendered something in its true character."

Camille Pissarro

What are these reindeer looking at? Is it the winter's night sky, an impressive tree, or an unexpected visitor?

"Since people are going to be living longer and getting older, they'll just have to learn how to be babies longer."

Andy Warhol

Draw four portraits of a man in four different stages of his life, from youth to old age.

"Angels fly because they take themselves lightly."
G. K. Chesterton

You may sometimes have the impression
that someone is watching over you, telling
you how to act or criticizing you . . .

*Try to draw your double,
your adviser, your guardian angel.*

"Many family trees started off as transplants."
Samuel Johnson

Draw your family tree.

Take advantage of family reunions to learn more about your ancestors and make your tree as big as possible.

*"If you want to make an apple pie from scratch,
you must first create the universe."*

Carl Sagan

Draw our good old planet

(the one that contains you, your friends and family, and,

somewhere far away, the author who made this book . . .)

Watch out,
it rotates!

"Shoot for the moon. Even if you miss, you'll land among the stars."
Les Brown

Like the Little Prince,
haven't you ever dreamed of other planets?

Draw the one you would like to escape to from time to time.

"I used to say that I would like to be someone; now I think I should have been more specific."

Anonymous

Me, ...,
7 months and 5 days after my first self-portrait.

Redo your self-portrait one last time as a "signature" in your workbook.

"A new year, a fresh start."
Christelle Heurtault

It's party time: Draw people talking, singing, and shouting with glee.

"Life is the best party."
Julia Child

Claude Lapointe thanks Éric Gasté, Tomi Ungerer, and Christian Voltz
for the use of their images in this book.

Day 6 © akg-images (left-hand image)
Day 82 © akg-images
Day 98 © Nimatallah/akg-images
Day 148 © akg-images
Day 203 © Brooklyn Museum of Art/Corbis
Day 219 © Erich Lessing/akg-images
Day 255 © Arte & Immagini srl/Corbis (left-hand image);
  © Collection Roger-Viollet (right-hand image)
Day 283 © Erich Lessing/akg-images

The Library of Congress has cataloged this book under
the Library of Congress Control Number 2007920792.
ISBN 13: 978-0-8109-9420-1
ISBN 10: 0-8109-9420-8

Copyright © 2006 Éditions de la Martinière,
an imprint of La Martinière Groupe, Paris
English translation copyright © 2007 Harry N. Abrams, Inc.
Translated by Gita Daneshjoo
Designed by Elisabeth Ferté

Printed and bound in Singapore
10 9 8 7 6 5 4 3 2 1

HNA
harry n. abrams, inc.
a subsidiary of La Martinière Groupe
115 West 18th Street
New York, NY 10011
www.hnabooks.com